Net Locality

Net Locality

Why Location Matters in a Networked World

Eric Gordon and
Adriana de Souza e Silva

WILEY-BLACKWELL

A John Wiley & Sons, Ltd., Publication

This edition first published 2011
© Eric Gordon and Adriana de Souza e Silva

Blackwell Publishing was acquired by John Wiley & Sons in February 2007. Blackwell's
publishing program has been merged with Wiley's global Scientific, Technical,
and Medical business to form Wiley-Blackwell.

Registered Office
John Wiley & Sons Ltd, The Atrium, Southern Gate, Chichester, West Sussex, PO19 8SQ,
United Kingdom

Editorial Offices
350 Main Street, Malden, MA 02148-5020, USA
9600 Garsington Road, Oxford, OX4 2DQ, UK
The Atrium, Southern Gate, Chichester, West Sussex, PO19 8SQ, UK

For details of our global editorial offices, for customer services, and for information about how
to apply for permission to reuse the copyright material in this book please see our website
at www.wiley.com/wiley-blackwell.

Library of Congress Cataloging-in-Publication Data
Gordon, Eric, 1973–
    Net locality : why location matters in a networked world / Eric Gordon and Adriana de Souza e Silva.
       p. cm.
    Includes bibliographical references and index.
    ISBN 978-1-4051-8061-0 (hardback) — ISBN 978-1-4051-8060-3 (paperback)
  1. Digital communications. 2. Integrated services digital networks. 3. Wireless communication
systems. 4. World Wide Web. 5. Internet—Technological innovations. 6. Digital communications—
Social aspects. I. Silva, Adriana de Souza e. II. Title.
    TK5103.75.G675 2011
    004.67′8—dc22   2011001785

A catalogue record for this book is available from the British Library.

This book is published in the following electronic formats: ePDFs (9781444340648);
Wiley Online Library (9781444340679); ePub (9781444340655)

Set in 10/12.5pt Galliard by Thomson Digital, Noida, India
Printed and bound in Malaysia by Vivar Printing Sdn Bhd

1   2011

para vovô Evandro (in memoriam) [Adriana]

Contents

Acknowledgments

It is a little ironic that two authors, each on a different continent, are writing a book about the importance of location. With one of us in Boston and the other moving between Raleigh, North Carolina and Copenhagen, Denmark, we have experienced the challenges that geographic distance can bring. And yet, through Twitter, instant messaging (IM), email, Skype, and various and sundry other technologies, we have worked together to write a book that is at once an analysis and testament to the power and flexibility of location in a networked world.

The challenges of physical distance were only compounded by the challenge of writing a book about a moving target. Just as we were trying to grasp the correspondence of our everyday writing schedules, we were trying to focus in on a topic that is changing at lightning pace. Location and location-based media are evolving so rapidly that we are sure that between now and when this book is actually published, we will be looking at a different world. So, in writing a book-length treatment on the topic, we knew we couldn't focus on the daily changes in the media landscape. We had to focus on the conceptual issues that bring all those little changes together. This book provides a perspective from which to view the emerging media landscape and imagine how it will transform in the years to come.

Like any project of this scope, we could not have accomplished what we did without a great deal of support. From the conversations we had in classrooms to the debates with colleagues, so many perspectives have influenced this book. But there are a few people who deserve special mention. We want to thank Steve Schirra for his tireless efforts in editing the final manuscript and providing substantive feedback. We asked for a little help and he gave a lot. He has been a great collaborator and friend throughout the process. We want to thank Jean Wang for her insights into the global context of net locality and her enormous help with crafting Chapter 7 and the conclusion of the book. We would also like to thank Jordan Frith for contributing to many of the ideas about locational privacy and surveillance present in Chapter 6. His insights on the personalization and control of public spaces through location-aware technologies were a great influence to that chapter. Finally, we want to thank Amani Naseem for her meticulous work in organizing and formatting the long list of references, as well as her work in securing permissions for the book's images. We too often forget how difficult it is to negotiate these details and how important it is to have talented and intelligent people near by to lend a helping hand. We also want to thank our home institutions, the IT University of Copenhagen, North Carolina State University, and Emerson College for providing financial and structural support during this process.

We owe a word of gratitude to Elizabeth Swayze, our editor at Wiley-Blackwell, who expressed interest in the project long ago and continued to champion it through thick and thin. She remained patient during its many delays and served as a careful reader of the manuscript and provided much needed feedback about style and tone.

We would also like to thank our family and friends. Although they did not directly contribute to the production of this book, they have provided us with lots of support. Specifically, I [Adriana] would like to thank my husband John Charles for his love and support during this process. Our long conversations about privacy and his input about the text were critical for the final outcome. And I [Eric] would like to thank my wife Justeen for her patience and insights, and my kids, Elliot and Adeline, for letting their dad obsess about something other than them for just a little while.

Finally, I [Adriana] would like to thank Eric for suggesting that we could combine efforts to write this book. Collaborations are never easy, but we were so eager to write this that the last year of work seems to have gone by really quickly. And I [Eric] would like to thank Adriana for bringing her critical insight and attention to detail to this project. In the spirit of true collaboration, the book is an amalgamation of our respective expertise that arose from spirited (and sometimes very spirited) deliberation.

Eric Gordon and Adriana de Souza e Silva
September 2010

Introduction

A man is walking down Michigan Avenue in Chicago. He shares a sidewalk with crowds of anonymous people. He sees skyscrapers and signage extending to the horizon. There is a lot going on – people talking, walking, playing, fighting, screaming, driving, and smiling. He sees a coffee shop that excites his interest. He pulls out his phone and checks into a location-based social network (LBSN). The application makes note of his location and registers his first stop of the day. He touches the "tips" tab on the application and looks at what other people have said about nearby locations and discovers that many have complained about its unfriendly service and high prices. While doing that, he gets notified that someone in his social network just checked into another coffee shop down the street. He walks over there to meet her.

The city for this man does not end with the visibly observable. It contains annotations and connections, information and orientations from a network of people and devices that extend well beyond what is in front of him. And he is not alone. It is difficult to find a mobile phone these days that is only a phone. Most phones send text messages, access the web, run applications, and include a Global Positioning System (GPS) receiver so that it can be located in the physical world. We used to talk about the World Wide Web as an interconnected information space set aside from the world we live in, but the world we live in and the web can no longer be so easily separated.

The spaces we interact with on a daily basis are filled with data – pictures, thoughts, reviews, and historical documentation – aggregated into accessible and usable bits of information. A Google search promptly uncovers thousands of references that are displayed according to the user's location.

Net Locality: Why Location Matters in a Networked World, First Edition. Eric Gordon and Adriana de Souza e Silva. © 2011 Eric Gordon and Adriana de Souza e Silva. Published 2011 by Blackwell Publishing Ltd.

A mobile phone, through any number of applications, can locate its user and find nearby relevant information. The technologies we use to access the web are location aware. The amount of online data, from websites and social networking sites (SNS) like Facebook and Twitter, to text messages and images, is growing exponentially. And, increasingly, that data is associated with its longitude and latitude coordinates so that it can be sorted not only by the who, what, and when – but also by the *where*. As location-aware phones become cheaper in much of the world, the number of people accessing and producing the world's data out *in the world* is expanding significantly.

The web instills locations with data resources, making those physical locations part of the web. There are millions of computers and mobile devices that are connected to each other and are discoverable by satellites. This is creating a near comprehensive map of where we are in relation to everything else. Our global networks of machines have made locating ourselves (and being located) so much easier. We are where our devices are, and we are perpetually leaving behind data traces that can be mapped to our physical world. So while we have always been location aware, and others have always been aware of our location, when we are immersed in information, being aware of locations has wholly new connotations.

This book is about an emerging form of location awareness we call *networked locality* (or net locality). It is about what happens to individuals and societies when virtually everything is located or locatable. More importantly, it is about what individuals and societies can do with the affordances of this location awareness – from organizing impromptu political protests to finding nearby friends and resources.

Net Locality

In January 2010 Google began integrating location data into all searches – either the location of an IP address of a desktop computer or the GPS coordinates of a phone now factors into search results. Many iPhone applications query the user about their location before they launch. Even if there is no obvious immediate use for location, the data is being collected and aggregated with a mind toward future value. The simple reality is that locally contextualized data is useful and convenient. It naturalizes a connection that was only metaphorical before. It takes the otherness of the web and places it squarely into where you are. No need to log on to the web, or even go someplace to access it. This is *net locality*. Net locality implies a ubiquity of networked information – a cultural approach to the web of information as intimately aligned with the perceptual realities of everyday life. We don't enter the web anymore; it is all around us. This is seductive. It promises to transcend the problems of joint custody – where we spend the week with physicality and the weekends with virtuality.

What net localities (the actual spaces where this is happening) mean for our institutions (government or education) our communities (neighborhoods or friends), and our spaces (cities or shopping malls) is the subject of this book. We describe a transition that will fundamentally alter what it means to be local in a globalizing world. Having access to a global network of information while situated within a local street, neighborhood, town, or city, potentially realigns how the individual deals with the scale of user experience. The street is no longer limited to the perceptual horizon of the person walking down it. A network of information that is accessible through a mobile device augments it. The provinciality of the small town, physically isolated from the rest of the world, is potentially cosmopolitan because of the integration of information into its streets. The way that geographers have traditionally understood the concept of scale is no longer accurate. Net locality renders geography more fluid, but never irrelevant, as was feared in the 1990s (Couclelis, 2007).

Likewise, geography becomes the organizational logic of the web. Our spaces of interaction can take place within multiple, simultaneous scales. The Yelp application (a location-based search and review service), for example, juxtaposes people and things that are nearby with an extended, potentially global network of information. While it prioritizes location in its search results, just as one might prioritize price in a traditional web search, it enables the user to move fluidly between that which is physically proximate and that which is conceptually proximate. The act of finding a nearby bagel shop is only a click away from reading about a bagel shop halfway around the world. This compression of scale is happening on a number of fronts, from browsing the web to attending a local neighborhood meeting, to using an augmented reality application to see, in a slightly new light, the street you have walked down a hundred times before.

Net locality, in general, is dependent upon the technological tools that make it possible. But, of course, tools are products of social needs. The hammer would not exist, for instance, if not for the need to press nails into wood. Likewise, GPS, radio frequency identification (RFID), Wi Fi triangulation, and other situating technologies have been adopted for web information storage and retrieval because of the social desire to locate ourselves in relation to information. Of course, once the tools are in place, they introduce new possibilities for use. A location-based game like Foursquare could not have been developed if not for GPS, web search,

Figure 0.1 Scene from *Minority Report* (de Bont, Curtis, Molen, Parkes, & Spielberg, 2002) where Tom Cruise's character walks into a GAP store and is greeted by an interactive billboard that knows his name and shopping history.

smart phones, and similar devices. Location awareness runs parallel to the technologies that enable it, and it is both a cause and a consequence of the use of these technologies.

But for most people, the thought of net locality is less evocative of pro-social developments, and more evocative of a dystopian surveillance society. Consider the scene in the film *Minority Report* (de Bont *et al.*, 2002) where Tom Cruise's character walks into a GAP store and an interactive billboard recognizes him, refers to him by name, and asks him how he is enjoying the shirts he purchased last week. We are quite comfortable with a targeted Google ad based on our search histories, but when that context aware advertising is transported into the physical world, it reflects a rather distressing breach of our perceived personal space. The circumstances of this scene are no longer science fiction. They are a reality. The technology to create this kind of interactive billboard is perfectly within reach. It remains speculative only because it breaches our current awareness of location and asks us to accept the ubiquity of net localities. So, while we are location aware, we are riddled with anxieties about it. In this book, we document the process of how the web has merged with our physical spaces and how it is transforming our everyday interactions with the world and each other.

Organizing the Web

Let's start with a story. In 1994, David Bohnett and John Rezner founded a web hosting company called Beverly Hills Internet (BHI). They started with a novel idea: using neighborhood names to organize and categorize web pages. Users, or "homesteaders" as they were called, were able to host their web pages for free within the virtual neighborhood of their choice. Each webpage was given a unique URL that included the name of the neighborhood and street address. The first neighborhoods bore names such as Coliseum, Hollywood, RodeoDrive, SunsetStrip, WallStreet, and WestHollywood. The idea was that users would gravitate to the neighborhood that best reflected their interests. For instance, an entertainment website would be in Hollywood, a financial site on WallStreet, and a music site on the SunsetStrip. And, in fact, these "neighborhoods" began to be quite important for people as they struggled to find a place on the web for their home pages. In December 1995, BHI had expanded to 14 neighborhoods, including Tokyo, Paris, and SiliconValley, and had officially changed its name to GeoCities.

GeoCities was purchased by Yahoo! in 1999 and fast became one of the largest web hosting sites in the world. The notion that the web could be organized by metaphorical neighborhoods was quite powerful. As the example of GeoCities shows, the early days of the web were ripe with the desire to neatly organize digital information in much the same way as we organize non-digital information: placing things in categories. David Weinberger, in his book *Everything is Miscellaneous* (2008), says that information can be ordered in one of three ways. The first order of order, as he calls it, is literally putting things into piles. For instance, in our dressers, most of us put socks in one drawer and shirts in another. This works surprisingly well. But what happens when we have too many socks to keep

Figure 0.2   GeoCities boasted 29 distinct neighborhoods in October 1996.

in a drawer? We need a different ordering system. Or, perhaps a better example would be, what happens when we have too many books to keep on a shelf? We create a log of book titles and authors, perhaps subjects, and we devise a categorizing system so that they are easily retrievable. The library card catalog is a prime example of the second order of order. GeoCities is another example of this second order. By placing links into categories, they were fixed into an ordering system that made intuitive sense. These websites (containing links to favorite song lyrics, pictures of cats, and family vacation photos) represented a model of interactivity now referred to as Web 1.0. According to Steven Johnson (2003), this was a very one-to-one kind of relationship: one person had the power to put up a link and another person had the power to decide whether or not to click on that link.[1]

With the quality of search engines in 1995 ranging from the manual (web rings) to the near useless (AltaVista), unless users put up links on their personal home pages to recommend particular websites, URLs had to be memorized. Around the end of the 1990s and early 2000s something began to change in the way people organized, created, and retrieved information online. The contemporary web (what is often referred to as Web 2.0) is organized in a more flexible ordering system than that. The third order of order is one that does not rely on fixed categories at all; the analog card catalog has been replaced by search engines like Google that parse through information in order to create usable and temporary results based on search algorithms. Entertainment websites, for instance, no longer need to be permanently placed into the "Hollywood" category to be findable. They can be found based on individual search terms and the particular context and preferences of the individual user. Digital information, Weinberger says, is "miscellaneous." A typical website is not placed in a finite number of categories determined by a content-management expert; it can be discovered through multiple terms and multiple platforms, such as web browsers, news aggregators, and smart phone apps.

Google was instrumental in reinventing this enormous amount of available data. The search engine contributed to transforming the web from an unwieldy database of carefully categorized information into a pile of miscellaneous information to be flexibly assembled. For instance, personal webpages with pictures of cats and favorite song lyrics no longer had to sit within the neighborhood of Silicon Valley. They could be found by searching for "cats" or the name of your favorite composer. Google made it okay for information to be miscellaneous – in fact, Google made it imperative that we don't fix information into categories.

In the 15 years since the development of GeoCities, the web has changed quite a bit. People are increasingly socializing, consuming entertainment and news, and searching for information online. We don't typically visit sites any longer. We simply visit *the web*. Tim O'Reilly has suggested that the web itself is the platform for engagement – no longer the individual site. We use aggregators or SNS to consume, produce, and share micro-content such as blog posts, tweets, and status updates.[2] The blog *post*, and not the blog, is the important unit of engagement. In short, the "places" we go on the web are all intimately connected, siphoned through our personal interests and machine aggregators. Because of the ubiquity of the web, we find that it is no longer constructive to distinguish between the web (often understood as content within web browsers) and the Internet, the infrastructure of networks that makes it all possible. It is *all* the web. Just like a television show is still television if viewed on the web, the web has become transcendent of its hardware and software and implies the web of content that pervades our communication landscape.

The web now extends to physical locations. When people have the opportunity to plot raw data onto collective maps (Berners-Lee, 2010) and to access the web from their location-aware mobile phones, there is, again, a critical change in how information is organized: from a "wasteland of unfiltered data" (Stoll, 1995) often referred to as "cyberspace," to a physically contextualized map of information. The new organizing logic of the web is based on physical location. Increasingly, the types of information we find and access online depend on where we are.

This connection to physical locations represents not only a new logic of organizing information online, but also a radical change in the very way we understand the web. GeoCities represented a way of thinking about the web that situated the world of information as wholly separate from the world of physical locations. There was, as Nicholas Negroponte (1995) famously put it, a clear distinction "between atoms and bits." What was possible in a world of pure information was very different from the possibilities of our physical world, limited by the laws of physics. Now, what is being organized is not just information, but the physical world that contains it.

Extending the web

The belief that the world of atoms was distinct from the world of bits was partly a consequence of the technologies we used to connect to the web. Using a stationary desktop computer to "enter" the web often meant that users had to be sitting down in front of a screen – a position that precluded many activities in the physical world. Additionally, the experience of surfing the web was often a solitary one. Even if the purpose for entering the web was to socialize with others, the popularization of virtual worlds and online chat rooms led many to think that we would end up communicating with each other primarily in digital spaces. This led to the belief that if the web could provide us with the feeling of "being somewhere," there would be no need to go out in public spaces and socialize with others face-to-face.

Half a decade after the invention of the first online virtual world (Richard Bartle and Roy Trubshaw's MUD), William Gibson's science fiction novel *Neuromancer* (1984) depicted an information world called the "Matrix" which users connected to via neural implants. In this world, one could literally "download their minds" and leave their physical bodies behind. Case, the main character in the novel, receives a penalty at the beginning of the story: he can no longer connect to cyberspace and is imprisoned in his own material body. Another character, Pov, is merely a "point of view," and is composed entirely of information, completely free from his material body. This notion persisted throughout the 1990s, represented in books such as Hans Moravec's *Mind Children* (1990) and movies like *Tron* (Kushner & Lisberger, 1983), *The Matrix* (Osbourne, Wachowski, & Wachowski, 1999) and *The Thirteenth Floor* (Emmerich *et al.*, 1999). These narrative references, coupled with an emerging academic field of Internet studies, established a paradigm of thinking about the web that was firmly ensconced in the notion that digital networks ran parallel to and remained separate from "real life."[3]

The possibility of socializing with people online prompted some to worry that vibrant public spaces would disappear. If one could do everything online – work, shop, bank, order food – why bother leaving the house? Undoubtedly, access to mobile phones and the mobile web has contributed to detaching people from their fixed work spaces and to performing activities on the move – such as talking, shopping, and coordinating with others. For these reasons, mobile phones were also frequently regarded as disconnecting people from their immediate physical location, and, more importantly, from social interactions in those locations. At some point, everyone has been inconvenienced by the use of mobile phones in restaurants, public transportation, and public spaces.

But this is more than just a nuisance. It has changed the way we think about the web. Information is not just miscellaneous; it is ubiquitous and located. The dominant metaphor for the web changed from virtuality to mobility. New studies reflected the changing methods by which users could interact with the communication network, and with each other, and although not a direct consequence of the popularity of location aware phones, the ability to do things (connecting with other people and information) while on the move challenged old assumptions about the status of physical spaces and the meaning of the web. What has been called the mobilities paradigm (Sheller & Urry, 2006) is not specifically about the web, but its emphasis on physical spaces and connectivity set the tone for a new way of thinking about the virtual/physical dichotomy. If during the 1990s being connected to the web meant staring at a fixed monitor, today being connected increasingly means walking through public spaces, looking at different advertisement screens, buying clothes, and talking to somebody on a mobile phone.

GeoCities officially closed its doors on October 26, 2009. The concept of the web as a metaphorical city has given way to the reality of the web as *part* of the city. As the world's information continues on its path to localization and searchability, as broadband and cellular networks become faster, and as portable devices become "smarter," the web has lost its distinction from the world it has sought to categorize. *References to physical space on the web (e.g., Hollywood, Silicon Valley) are no longer metaphors for digital information; physical space has become the context for that information.* We can no longer talk about our "real" lives and our digital lives. We can only talk about the interfaces through which our various communication channels (face-to-face, email, SMS, and many others) come together. In the 1990s the idea of the "virtual city" dominated people's imaginations (Donath, 1997; Mitchel, 1995), but today, there is no digital city of the web; rather, for most people, there is no physical city without the web.

Location Awareness

Location-based services (LBS) comprise the fastest growing sector in web technology businesses with a forecasted profit growth from $515 million in 2007 to $13.3 billion in 2013 (ABI Research, 2009). And within LBS, personal navigation – services that allow users to access and share location and information with friends – is the fastest growing area. The incorporation of location data into social and business applications shows no signs of letting up. In December 2009, Twitter announced that it would make available the location data of tweets. In March 2010, Facebook announced that it would begin attaching location data to status updates through what was called Facebook Places. And the Google answer to social networking, Buzz, was launched in 2010 with location-aware functionality. The availability of locational data leads to applications like GeoChirp or TwitterMap, which contextualize tweets by geographical coordinates, or TwittARound, an augmented reality map that blends the camera feature on a smart phone with localized tweets.

Figure 0.3 GeoChirp interface at www.geochirp.com. A product of Cue Blocks Technologies Pvt Ltd. 2010 Cue Blocks Technologies Pvt Ltd. All rights reserved. Reproduced by permission of Cue Blocks Technologies Pvt Ltd.

Figure 0.4 TwittARound interface for the iPhone. Reproduced by permission of Michael Zöllner.

While these applications, and all the applications we discuss in this book, are likely to change, we want to draw attention to what they do and how they do it. So, even if they are no longer around or have completely shifted in their state of perpetual beta, these examples can be abstracted to address their broader function.

Location is an increasingly useful form of data aggregation for the desktop accessible web browser, but it is *foundational* to mobile applications. It is now evident that one of the main characteristics of mobile (smart) phones is their ability to locate and contextualize one's engagement with the web.[4] For example, LBSNs such as Foursquare or Loopt allow users to see the location of their "friends" on their mobile phone screens. Likewise, location-based advertising can deliver coupons whenever a user is within a certain distance of specific stores,[5] and mobile annotation applications such as WikiMe, GeoGraffiti, and Google Maps mashups allow individuals to access and upload information that is place specific. Because users can customize the types of information they are willing to interact with (which friends they would like to see, which coupons they want to receive, what information they want to access), people can now use these devices to personalize and control their experiences of physical spaces. The physical world is ripe with information; web users can organize that information around where they happen to be.

The database is all around us. While this scenario opens up some exciting possibilities for new forms of interacting with the world and each other, it is not difficult to imagine the corresponding dangers. One of the consequences of being able to locate things and people is that you can also be located, and frequently location-aware technologies have been viewed with skepticism and fear due to possible threats to personal privacy and the imminence of top-down and collateral surveillance.

As people become more comfortable with letting their devices track their longitude and latitude coordinates, as they grow accustomed to the location of their IP address informing search results, and as they come to expect locally relevant advertising, they are opening themselves up to the environment. Surveillance is more than just hidden cameras and undercover police officers; environments track us through our voluntary exposure of personal data. When Roger Clarke (1988) introduced the notion of dataveillance (or data surveillance) in 1988, he was referring mostly to the surreptitious tracking of personal data through centralized machines. But now, location-aware devices normalize dataveillance and make it a necessary component of our everyday interactions with the web. The sharing of data is essential for us to properly "use" the web.

Mapping information and people provides the infrastructure from which the user can be placed in relative distance to the mapped world. But we are not suggesting that users necessarily feel closer to the world mapped. The philosopher Martin Heidegger (1971) noted in the 1950s that radio technology does not bring the world closer. Listening to the voice of the broadcaster, while it seems so intimately near, as though in the same room, is in fact just the misunderstanding of the lack of distance. People often turn on the radio when they feel lonely; but there is no intimacy in hearing that voice, only the impression of intimacy. That intimacy is, in large part, manufactured.

In actual practice, physical proximity and mediated proximity have very different implications for how people behave. Two people sitting next to each other on a bus, for example, have a responsibility for each other that one person listening to another on the radio does not. If the person sitting next to you cuts his arm when sitting down, you would probably ask how he is doing; however, if the voice on the radio describes a similar misfortune, you would not likely call the station to inquire about her well being. Distance becomes clear when we are reminded of presence in physical location.

But, as location aware technologies and practices transform how people become aware of their location, the distinction between nearness and distancelessness is growing thin. Broadcast media manufactures the feeling of intimacy by making it seem as though the radio announcer is in the room talking to you. This goes one way. The radio announcer likely does not feel the same way about all the potential listeners of a program. But, plotting oneself in location relative to the observed world challenges the hard and fast distinction between what appears near through mediation and what actually *is* near (Couldry & Markham, 2008). When one is inserted into a map and placed into a geographical relationship to things mapped, there is a sense of distancelessness, in that there appears to be universal access to everything, but there is also a sense of nearness, in that everything is measured in actual distance from the observer.

Increasingly, locating oneself is not merely a form of participation, like adding a comment to a blog or posting a review on Yelp. It literally sets the conditions for interaction and provides the context from which information is interpreted and used. Location, therefore, is of greater significance then other forms of networked identity. Usernames and avatars construct identity (Turkle, 1995; Donath, 1997), but location constructs the framework through which identity can be formed. It positions the user within a network: not just as a member of an online community, but in relation to the network more generally. The radical visibility of located data creates the *potentiality* for users to experience meaningful nearness to things and people (Couldry & Markham, 2008; Scannell, 1996). The transformation of mediated social interaction from mere distancelessness, as Heidegger called it, to nearness is a matter of practice.

Reading the Book

The web has not fully permeated every aspect of our lives, but there has been a breach in the dam, and networked data is flooding into our physical spaces. This flood is spurred by new technologies; however, the desire to connect information to location well precedes the technologies we are currently using.

The first technology to deliberately facilitate location awareness is the map. Rather than writing a history of mapmaking, in the first chapter we look instead to the particular practices of social mapping – or the use of maps to accomplish collective goals. We examine a history of social mapping practices from the cholera outbreak in London to early experiments with geographic information systems (GIS) to web-based mapping, which normalized the activity of mapping information and people into everyday life. We examine how Google Maps, which, in addition to functioning as a wayfinding tool, has transformed web searching in general. Location has become central to the way we navigate information, and as a result, has become central to the way we expect to be navigated.

Mobile devices are the primary tools with which we access location. Much of the located data being produced is coming from mobile, location-aware technologies. With GPS and cell triangulation continuously recording location data in most handheld devices, the function of contextualizing information into physical space is automated. Though new "smart" phones like the iPhone and Android have had a great deal to do with popularizing location-aware technologies, in Chapters 2 and 3 we point to a history of art and research projects, from spatial annotation tools to location-based games, that have influenced the current condition of location awareness. While Chapter 2 focuses on mobile annotation projects – the ability of attaching information to locations – Chapter 3 discusses the development of LBSNs, showing how social interaction in net localities is increasingly dependent upon the user's location. This rich history of experimentation demonstrates our position that net locality is not the product of specific technologies, but is instead emerging out of a cultural need to contextualize ourselves within a growing network of information.

This has big implications for cities. Chapter 4 looks to what's happening in cities and how these tools and practices are changing public spaces and interactions. Urban spaces are becoming hybridized (de Souza e Silva, 2006), meaning they are composed through a combination of physical and digital practices. For each individual, the urban environment is constructed through perceptions of nearby information and people; the experience of net locality translates what we understand as near, and how we understand the co-presence of other individuals. Noting someone's presence in a location-based mobile game, or tracking somebody's located updates on a LBSN alters one's perceptions of the composition and boundaries of the environment. While we are careful not to wholeheartedly celebrate these alterations in the conditions of urban public spaces, we believe that it is important to construct a framework from which to scrutinize them that is distinct from our traditional understanding of what makes "good public spaces."

So what does this do for the way we interact in our communities and participate in the public sphere? Being aware of the dynamics of a location can empower users to act within them. In Chapter 5 we ask how net localities are transforming community interaction, local politics, and civic engagement. From community listservs to hyperlocal blogs to government sponsored "participation tools," the landscape of local participation is being altered. Who gets to participate and in what capacity is an open question, one that grassroots organizations, civic innovators, and city governments are seeking to answer. Of course, location awareness is not available to everyone; the digital divide is a real issue as net localities become the platform for public policy.

Just as the public sphere is being reorganized, so is the private sphere. Put plainly, networked devices are able to track their users' locations. Private companies and government agencies are collecting location data to track major trends; users are tracking their "friend's" data to foster connections and keep tabs on them. This form of surveillance is challenging traditional notions of privacy. We argue in Chapter 6 that in light of net locality, we need to wholly reconsider what privacy means. LBS is the fastest growing web sector because people are increasingly comfortable with disclosing their location as long as they feel as though they are gaining something from that disclosure. Contextualizing oneself in the expansive digital network is that payoff, and it is framed as a reasonable sacrifice only if the individual user feels as though they have control over the extent of their disclosure and the people to whom they disclose. And still, most people have no idea what service providers do with the location information they collect.

The examples we use throughout this book are mostly drawn from the United States and Western Europe. It would be far too ambitious for us to suggest that this phenomenon is universally applicable throughout the world. That said, in Chapter 7, we attempt to extend our argument to other cultural contexts by looking specifically at two Asian countries – China and Japan. The practices we describe in the United States and Western Europe, and the norms of behavior constructed around them, are not universally applicable. Every culture carries unique assumptions about privacy and publicity, social life and governmentality. By looking at the nuances of perceptions that influence technology adoption, we suggest a framework through which to understand net localities in a global context. This chapter is not meant to be an extensive study of two countries; instead, it is meant to argue *against* the universality of our claims. Net locality is, indeed, a global phenomenon, but it needs to be considered locally. How specific cultures appropriate technologies, adapt social practices, and produce cultural references, are going to influence the meanings of location.

Finally, in the conclusion, we consider the future of net locality and location awareness more generally. The technological infrastructure is being built throughout the world, including a global 4G cellular network that will fundamentally alter how most people engage with the web. It is faster and better able to accommodate inter-device communication. Your phone and your computer will no longer exist in little silos. Devices, including your television set and gaming console, will become access points to a ubiquitous, contextualized network. Of course there are social implications to this level of connectivity. For instance, as we have already mentioned, the technology is already available to allow customized advertisements to be pushed directly to your mobile device that would refer to where you are and what you have purchased recently. But the social norms do not yet exist to make these technologies widely acceptable. We will become more location aware as technological networks expand their influence into every part of our lives. The question remains, however, as to whether or not this awareness will compromise or enhance our personal freedoms and capacity to act in a complex and networked world.

Notes

1   However, the type of interactivity that captured the "web zeitgeist of 1995" (Johnson, 2003) was far away from the original models for organizing and retrieving information envisioned by World Wide Web pioneers Vannevar Bush, Ted Nelson, and Tim Berners-Lee. In his seminal article "As we may think,"

Bush (1945) proposed a revolutionary way of organizing information that followed the way our thinking works: by association, rather than by hierarchy. For Bush, putting things into categories, like an encyclopedia does, was not only counterproductive (because it didn't match how we connect our thoughts), it would also not be capable of accessing and retrieving the increasing amount of information available. About 20 years later, Ted Nelson (1965), following Bush's ideas, proposed a computer system he called Xanadu, which allowed the non-sequential linking of electronic documents. Based on Bush's and Nelson's visions of organizing information by association, Tim Berners-Lee (Berners-Lee *et al.*, 1994) first designed the World Wide Web.

2   SNS have enabled an ease and flexibility of information sharing. As of 2009, more than 55% of US teens (ages 12–17) and 75% of adults (ages 18–24) were using SNS, and nearly 60% of news consumers were getting some or all of their news online. More specifically, a report from the Pew Internet and American Life Project contends that news consumption is "portable, personalized and participatory," with 33% of mobile phone owners getting their news on their mobile phones; 28% of Internet users having customized their home pages for delivering news; and 37% of Internet users having commented on or disseminated news via Facebook or Twitter (Purcell *et al.*, 2010).

3   For more on this topic, see Turkle, 1995; Castells, 2000; Negroponte, 1995.

4   For a more detailed analysis of this concept, see: Humphreys, 2007; de Souza e Silva, 2006, 2009; de Souza e Silva and Sutko, 2009; Gordon, 2008.

5   Target released an iPhone app for just this purpose in early 2010.

References

ABI Research. (2009). *Applications, platforms, positioning technology, handset evolution, and business model migration.* Retrieved November 1, 2010 from http://www.abiresearch.com/research/1003335-Mobile+Location+Based +Services

Berners-Lee, T., (2010, March). Tim Berners-Lee: The year open data went worldwide [Video]. *TED Talks.* Retrieved November 1, 2010, from http://www.ted.com/talks/lang/eng/tim_berners_lee_the_year_open_data _went_worldwide.html

Berners-Lee, T., Caillou, R., Luotonen, A., Nielsen, F., & Secret, A. (1994). The World Wide Web. *Communications of the ACM, 37*(8), 907–912. Also available in Wardrip-Fruin, N., & Montfort, N. (Eds.). (2003). *The new media reader* (pp. 791–798). Cambridge, MA: MIT Press.

Bush, V. (1945). As we may think. *Atlantic Monthly, 176*(1), 101–108.

Castells, M. (2000). *The rise of the network society.* Oxford: Blackwell.

Clarke, R. (1988). Information technology and dataveillance. *Communications of the ACM, 31*(5), 498–512.

Couclelis, H. (2007). Misses, near-misses and surprises in forecasting the informational city. In Miller, H. J. (Ed.), *Societies and cities in the age of instant access* (pp. 70–83). Dordrecht, The Netherlands: Springer.

Couldry, N., & Markham, T., (2008). Troubled closeness or satisfied distance? Researching media consumption and public orientation. *Media, Culture, Society, 30*(1), 5–21.

de Bont, J., Curtis, B., Molen, G., & Parkes, W. F., (Producers), & Spielberg, S., (Director) (2002). *Minority report* [Motion picture]. United States: Amblin Entertainment, Cruise/Wagner Productions.

de Souza e Silva, A. (2006). Cyber to hybrid: Mobile technologies as interfaces of hybrid spaces. *Space and Culture, 9*(3), 261.

de Souza e Silva, A. (2009). Hybrid reality and location-based gaming: Redefining mobility and game spaces in urban environments. *Simulation & Gaming, 40*(3), 404.

de Souza e Silva, A., & Sutko, D. M. (2009). *Digital cityscapes: Merging digital and urban playspaces*. New York: Peter Lang.

Donath, J. (1997). *Inhabiting the virtual city* (Unpublished PhD dissertation). Massachusetts Institute of Technology, Cambridge, MA. Retrieved November 1, 2010, from http://smg.media.mit.edu/people/judith/Thesis/IllustConv.frame.html

Emmerich, R., Emmerich, U., Weber, M. (Producers), & Rusnak, J. (Director). (1999). *The thirteenth floor* [Motion Picture]. United States: Columbia Pictures/Centropolis Entertainment.

Gibson, W. (1984). *Neuromancer*. New York: Berkley.

Gordon, E. (2008). Towards a theory of network locality. *First Monday 13*(10). Retrieved November 1, 2010, from http://firstmonday.org/htbin/cgiwrap/bin/ojs/index.php/fm/article/view/2157/20

Heidegger, M. (1971). The thing. *Poetry, language, thought*. New York: Harper and Row.

Humphreys, L. (2007). Mobile social networks and social practice: A case study of dodgeball. *Journal of Computer-Mediated Communication, 13*(1), 341–360. DOI: 10.1111/j.1083–6101.2007.00399.x

Johnson, S. (2003). The web as a city [Video]. *TED talk*. Retrieved November 1, 2010, from http://www.ted.com/talks/lang/eng/steven_johnson_on_the_web_as_a_city.html

Kushner, D. (Producer), & Lisberger, S. (Director). (1983). *Tron* [Motion picture]. United States: Walt Disney Pictures/Lisberger Studios.

Mitchel, W. (1995). *City of bits, space, place, and the Infobahn*. Cambridge, MA: MIT Press.

Moravec, H. (1990). *Mind children: The future of robot and human intelligence*. Cambridge, MA: Harvard University Press.

Negroponte, N. (1995). *Being digital*. New York: Vintage Books.

Nelson, T. H. (1965). Complex information processing: A file structure for the complex, the changing, and the indeterminate. In Winner, L. (Ed.),

Proceedings of the 1965 20th National Conference: Association for Computing Machinery, pp. 84–100. New York: ACM Press. DOI: 10.1145/800197.806036

Osbourne, B. (Producer), Wachowski, A., & Wachowski, L. (Directors). (1999). *The matrix* [Motion picture]. United States: Warner Brothers, and Australia: Village Roadshow Pictures/Silver Pictures.

Purcell, K., Rainie, L., Mitchell, A., Rosentiel, T., & Olmstead, K. (2010). *Understanding the participatory news consumer. Pew internet and American life project*. Washington, DC: Pew Research Center.

Scannell, P. (1996). *Radio, television and modern life*. Oxford: Blackwell.

Sheller, M., & Urry, J. (2006). The new mobilities paradigm. *Environment and Planning A, 38*(2), 207–226.

Stoll, C. (1995). The Internet? Bah! Hype alert: Why cyberspace isn't, and will never be, Nirvana. *Newsweek*. Retrieved November 1, 2010, from http://www.newsweek.com/id/106554

Turkle, S. (1995). *Life on the screen: Identity in the age of the internet*. New York: Simon & Schuster.

Weinberger, D. (2008). *Everything is miscellaneous*. New York: Henry Holt.

1

Maps

Lior Ron, the Google product manager for GeoSearch, announced at the Where 2.0 Conference in May 2008 that we should no longer think about Google Maps. Instead, he explained proudly, we need to think about Google *on* maps. This subtle turn of phrase suggests the transition from an isolated web application with a particular functionality to a whole new way of thinking about search. Most information is located or locatable; the map, according to Ron, could become the universal interface from which to access that information. He illustrated his point by announcing three new Google Maps features: toggles to view Wikipedia articles, photos, and news feeds. With these features turned on, the map indeed transforms from a wayfinding tool to a search interface. And this was just the tip of the iceberg, he informed the audience: as more and more location information is automatically generated by Global Positioning System (GPS) or Wi-Fi technologies, unlocated information will cease to be the norm. Digital pictures are already mostly marked with their longitude and latitude (longlat) coordinates on sites like Flickr and Picasa; news stories are tied to specific cities, neighborhoods, even blocks; and blog entries are tied to location of upload and location of content, as is the case of most mobile blogs (or moblogs). More recently, Blaise Agüera y Arcas (2010), the architect of Bing Maps at Microsoft, demonstrated a mapping application that transforms online maps into 3D landscapes depending on the user's zoom level. The real innovation of Bing Maps is that it allows users not only to retrieve any kind of geotagged information – as is common with Google Maps – but also to access live video streams from street cameras. Bing Maps also allows users to access video streaming from indoor cameras. So not only

Net Locality: Why Location Matters in a Networked World, First Edition. Eric Gordon and Adriana de Souza e Silva. © 2011 Eric Gordon and Adriana de Souza e Silva. Published 2011 by Blackwell Publishing Ltd.

are outside spaces becoming mapped, but indoor places as well. As the geolocation infrastructure continues to build out, location becomes a near universal search string for the world's data.

There is a growing industry built around the process of locating information. The Where 2.0 Conference, one of the industry's primary convergence points, was established in 2005 by O'Reilly Media as a means of harnessing the industrial energies behind the new possibilities opened up by the collision of location technologies and the web. For many decades, the geolocation industry was focused on developing high-end geographic information system (GIS) software for market and social research, as well as military purposes. But when Google Maps launched in February 2005, and its application programming interface (API) was made available to the public just a few months later, the specialized domain of GIS programmers became the domain of everyday users. The geographer Michael Goodchild said of the new Google software: "It's like the effect of the personal computer in the 1970s, where previously there was quite an elite population of computer users. Just as the PC democratized computing, so systems like [these] will democratize GIS" (Butler, 2006). Plotting information on maps, in what has become known as Google Maps mashups, is now a common practice. From the moment Google released its API, maps about everything from crime to real estate to entertainment began circulating around the web. While Google was not necessarily the first to the mapping game, it was instrumental in spurring a popularization of mapping practices.

What started as a useful tool, and then perpetuated an amateur practice, has turned into a sizable industry. The geolocation industry, once focused exclusively on tools for mapping information for specific purposes, has turned to tools that automate or encourage users to provide location metadata on all information so that maps can obtain a more broad-spectrum function. The new industry is built on the premise that web mapping is the future of a spatialized search – a future premised on longlat coordinates being as commonplace as file names.

Many terms have been employed to describe this phenomenon: the geospatial web (Kohn, 1970; Scharl & Tochtermann, 2007), neogeography (Turner, 2006), Web Mapping 2.0 (Haklay, Singleton, & Parker, 2008). But these terms are employed typically to describe the technologies or the unique goals of using them, and not the social and phenomenal processes of interacting with networked spaces. The geospatial web – or the geoweb – describes the infrastructure necessary for web mapping, neogeography means 'new geography' and describes the wide spread practices that make-up the participatory geoweb, and Web Mapping 2.0 sets out to combine these things to define the viewing practices of an emerging medium. What has not been properly addressed, however, is how this new context for geographical knowledge production through web mapping is doing more than transforming mapping practices; it is transforming communication more broadly. Net locality implies a different way of knowing and experiencing space, not just a different tool for visualization.

But maps are not new. Even before localities were networked, maps were employed to make sense of information in physical spaces. Ptolemy, the Greek philosopher and mathematician writing in the second century AD, declared in the opening lines of his *Geographia* that maps are "a representation in picture of the whole known world together with the phenomena which are contained therein" (Ptolemy, 1991). They were not just flat pictures of space; they were to be representations of everything that could be located. But, of course, cartographers did not have the necessary technology to realize this vision. Accurately representing geographic boundaries was itself a difficult and labor-intensive process that required long expeditions and teams of people. Mapping the changing landscape of commerce or the intricate relations between people was well beyond what maps could do. However, technological developments, particularly in the last century, have pushed mapping closer to the center of everyday life. And while there has always been a compulsion to organize information in terms of physical localities, it is only recently that this has manifested itself in such an obvious and dramatic way. Now that we are immersed in data, the map is the most logical framework through which to make sense of it. In this chapter, we will talk about how maps have changed from single-function wayfinding tools to multi-function tools for the personal navigation of society, politics and culture.

Mapping Social Information

In 1854, London experienced its most significant cholera outbreak. Hundreds of people were falling ill and dying in neighborhoods throughout the city. During the panic, the miasma theory prevailed: bad air, from rancid slaughterhouses or factories, was causing people to contract the intestinal infection, as bad smells were tantamount to diseased air. A physician by the name of John Snow, however, doubted this theory, instead claiming that germs in the drinking water were causing the cholera outbreak. He first attempted to prove this theory by identifying these microscopic troublemakers, but his analysis under the microscope was inconclusive. Despite the logic of his claims, the germ theory received little traction in the mainstream science community. Few were willing to give up on the miasma theory. But Snow was so convinced it was the drinking water, that he set out on an unprecedented effort to prove his case. He ventured into the "diseased air" along with the Reverend Henry Whitehead, and knocked on doors to inquire about where people got their drinking water. After canvassing the neighborhood, Whitehead and Snow began plotting their data on a map of the city. He noticed that there was a significant concentration of cases in close proximity to a well on Broad Street. The people who were using this well to get their drinking water were far more likely to have contracted the disease. Where the microscope failed, the map provided conclusive evidence, which compelled the local council (until then, firm advocates of the miasma theory) to disable the well by removing its handle.

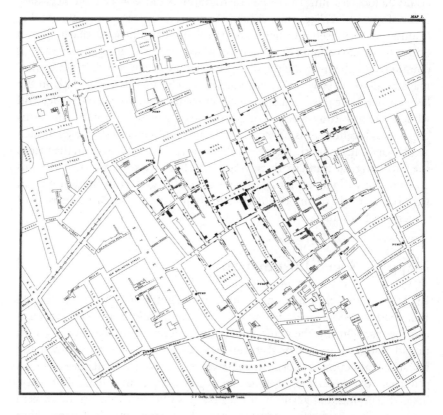

Figure 1.1 Snow and Whitehead's representation of cholera cases on a map of London in 1854. The map was first published in John Snow's book *On the Mode of Communication of Cholera*, 1855.

Through the spatial visualization of social information, Snow and Whitehead were able to persuade a doubting public and scientific community to think in a completely different way. The map as a tool for social understanding was pushed into the spotlight, jumpstarting the nascent discipline of epidemiology and foregrounding a new use for cartography (Merril & Timmreck, 2006). Instead of mere direction, maps were proven useful in determining relation. The data was contained within geographic coordinates, and once plotted, it illuminated proximity from point to point. With an underground sewage system as extensive as London's that had circuitous correlations between sources, pipes, and wells, implicating the Broad Street well was quite an accomplishment. Snow's map demonstrated how the neighborhood divided between many different wells, and proximity to the Broad Street well was predictive, but not determinative of deaths from the disease. By going door to door and talking to people, Snow and Whitehead learned that some people, even those who lived closest to the Broad Street well, might have retrieved their water elsewhere if it was more convenient to work or family. It wasn't just locating the dead that made the map so important – it was the mapping of social information, carefully collected and displayed, that sparked a new era of cartography (Tufte, 1997).

Since Snow's innovation, the mapping of social or ecological information has become common practice in the burgeoning fields of epidemiology, landscape architecture, urban planning and other forms of social or natural research. Simply overlaying data on top of a geographical representations, what became known as the "layered cake" capability, proved useful and persuasive for a range of purposes. One of the breakthrough moments in layered cake mapping was the geographer John K. Wright's use of overlays for mapping population densities on Cape Cod (1936). By combining population data alongside data from the US Geological Survey, Wright was able to identify patterns in uninhabited land on the Cape to help determine its environmental and social impacts. This early work led Wright to reflect on the importance of combining maps with social information. In a 1947 article, Wright identified something called *cartographic geosophy*: "The cartographic approach to geosophy involves the making of maps that present information about the distribution of geographical knowledge. Obviously, every map tells us something in this regard; a geosophic map is one designed specifically for the purpose." The notion that some maps were produced primarily to spatialize information, as opposed to provide information about space, was vastly important in the evolution of cartography. The plotting of population densities on a map in order to characterize per capita income distributions is quite different than plotting the location of rivers and streams. The first uses the geographic lens to illuminate the data set, and the latter uses data to illuminate the geography. Wright further divided cartographic geosophy into two categories. The first is a map that presents information about what is or has been known about different geographical areas, including something such as the geographical survey of population density we mentioned above, or even opinion research. This is mapping social information. The second category was speculative. This might include the collective plotting of opinions or attitudes, where user data is not extracted by an expert but produced by the users themselves. For the mappers and the mapped, the difference is in interacting with information that is not yet known – it comes into being through the collective process of mapping. But "whether or not this particular geosophic map would be either feasible or desirable," Wright concluded, "geosophic maps in general bring out sharply the contrast between the shadows of ignorance and the light of knowledge" (1947). In other words, maps not only clarify what we already know; they present the conditions for the reframing of questions. This second category of geosophic map is not a finished document, but a stage whereby the mapper and the mapped enter into an ongoing conversation about a specific topic framed by geographical space. This concept was essential in guiding the development of maps into computing environments. In the 1960s, the data crunching power of new mainframe computers quite literally transformed what a map could be.

GIS: Converging Maps and Computers

In the early 1960s, Roger Tomlinson, a cartographer who had gone to work for the Canadian Agricultural Rehabilitation and Development Administration, was tasked with the job of automating its mapping services. In partnership with IBM, Tomlinson helped develop the Canadian Geographic Information System (CGIS). This was the first implementation of what is now known as GIS. Tomlinson's motivation for developing such a system was simple: hardcopy maps had significant limitations. First, only a certain amount of descriptive data could be shown on a single map. According to Tomlinson (1998), "The data content of hardcopy maps is limited by size of sheet on which the information is recorded and the space required by each item of data so that it remains legible" (p. 22). The computer could change all that by offering near infinite flexibility in display while at the same time hard coding data analysis into the parameters of longitude and latitude. Also, the hardcopy map had to be read and analyzed by a human. "To store a large amount of data on maps, you have to produce many maps. To extract information visually from a very large number of maps represents a formidable task of reading and measurement" (1998, p. 22). The computer could automate data analysis, vastly expanding the scope of mappable datasets.

While CGIS introduced the possibility of integrating computers and maps, much of the significant innovation in this field came out of universities. Most notably, the work of Howard Fisher served to legitimize the field of study. While Fisher was an architect in Chicago in the 1960s, he worked with some computer programmers to produce a synagraphic mapping tool (SYMAP) – a system that could assimilate points, lines and areas as input into a dynamic map. After receiving significant financial support from the Ford Foundation to continue work on the project, in 1965 he moved to Cambridge, Massachusetts to set up the Laboratory for Computer Graphics at the Graduate School of Design at Harvard University. This center became a hub for computerized cartography, with dozens of graduate students and staff working to enhance SYMAP as well as developing other systems. By the end of the 1960s, SYMAP was widely distributed to various institutions, universities, and organizations in the public and private sectors. By that time, universities throughout North America and the United Kingdom, including the Experimental Cartography Unit (ECU) at the Royal College of Art, the University of Oregon, and the University of Kansas, were directing their efforts toward producing new systems that offered significant advances in photogrammetry and topological analysis as well as cultivating the methodological aspects of quantitative geography, including what became known as geostatistics. GIS was sophisticated enough for the technologies and data extraction methodologies to have a significant presence in all of the spatial disciplines – urban planning, epidemiology, architecture, geography, and ecology. But it certainly wasn't limited to academic work. By the 1980s, the needs of municipalities, market researchers, and the military turned GIS into a multi-billion dollar industry (Peng & Tsou, 2003).

Web GIS

By the late 1990s, the ability to deliver GIS tools or products over the web changed the social utility of mapping. What was conceived as a tool for professionals to process professionally accumulated datasets for the purpose of professional analysis could now be widely disseminated over the web (Peng & Tsou, 2003). Web GIS emerged not long after the web itself.

The Xerox PARC Map Viewer was introduced in 1993 and enabled the retrieval of localized maps via hyperlinks. Specialized applications continued to build, and by the mid-1990s the Open Geospatial Consortium (OGC) set standards of cartographic interoperability, so that individual developers of web GIS could share geographic data. Companies like ESRI, taking advantage of newly open data sources, were central in the wide spread proliferation of GIS over the web. Public organizations and governments quickly adopted these tools to make data available to constituents. There was a clear market for location services. It wasn't just that this technology was being foisted on the public; the public wanted to know where things were. For example, Ontario, California opened up its municipal databases for public consumption, making it possible for people to access official maps of property lines and utility service routes. In 1997, the textile towns of Cabarrus County, North Carolina made all of their public land records available on the web. Users could search for any parcel, retrieve records of its ownership history and zoning, as well as tax records. Web dissemination allowed for the rarified objects of GIS processes to be accessible to everyday consumers. According to Christian Harder (1998), this shift in dissemination would have significant implications for society. In response to those who claim that the web doesn't change the fundamental nature of GIS, but only gets it online, Harder rebuts that that is "comparable to saying that a printing press doesn't change the fundamental nature of a book. The value of geographic information (like all forms of digital information) and the power of GIS applications to solve problems," he claims, "are proportional to their accessibility" (1998, p. 1). In homes and offices throughout the world, the web made it possible for people to access computer generated maps to learn about their cities or neighborhoods, to obtain driving directions, or to plot social networks. Whatever the content of these maps, the sheer possibility for online distribution would reframe the GIS debate once again. Accessibility does not only concern the number of people who access a specific technology; it is also related to how the technology changes social practices and local cultures. Returning to the example of the book, in her extensive study about the impact of the printing press in modern Europe, historian Elizabeth Eisenstein (1979) points out how the ease of publishing generated a greater number of books in languages other than Latin, which ultimately contributed to many counties adopting the local vernacular as their official language. Consequently more people could be taught how to read, which increased literacy. Additionally, the ability to access several (contradictory) copies of the same works influenced the development of modern science (following a culture of skepticism and empiricism) and eventually led to the protestant reformation. Likewise, the greater accessibility to GIS over the web not only changed the nature of what we understand as GIS, but also the very nature of GIS as an interface, which shapes new ways through which we interact with localized information.

Not everyone considered this widespread dissemination of GIS a good thing (Foresman, 1998). Some critics doubted whether this computational form of mapping could enhance any knowledge whatsoever. While GIS proponents often adopted terms like freedom, opportunity, empowerment, communication, and democracy to signal their continued faith in the benign role of the technology, opponents used terms such as control, exploitation, unsavory constraint, faceless, and elitist (Clark, 1998). The central thrust of the criticism was that through the automated plotting of social information on maps, the subjects that produced the original data are objectified and reduced to mere data points. Critics claimed that GIS functions by abstracting complex human subjectivity into a machine to be processed and generalized, thus working against the foundational pre-suppositions of liberal democracy.[1] While the practical effects of this criticism did not seem to have much of an effect on the booming GIS industry, it served to frame the academic debate about GIS around questions of democracy and humanism. What's at stake when one's personal data is compiled and mapped onto a representation of space? If the individual components of one's life – ethnicity, income, political beliefs – can be mapped in myriad ways to prove varying points, then what power is sacrificed by making one's data available? Was the power of personal agency shattered by the possibility of computerized mapping? Does it harden the division between the mapper and the mapped? But the web promised to dissolve many of these concerns. No longer a document to be analyzed by a group of experts, the web-GIS map could communicate widely; it went from scientific document to cultural logic. It removed location from the purview of experts and placed it in the hands of everyday people.

Jacek Malczewski (2004) describes three major phases of GIS development: first, the research frontier period, 1950s–1960s; second, the integration period where general purpose GIS get employed into many scientific contexts, 1970s–1980s; and third, the proliferation stage which marks a shift to user-oriented GIS on the web, 1990s. Indeed, by 1998, searching for driving directions, locating a business, or tracking weather patterns were some of the most popular things to do with network connectivity (Peterson, 1999). The web enabled users to pull geographical information at their whim. But it did not yet introduce the desire to *push* geographical information, or what Michael Goodchild (2007) calls "volunteered geographical information." As more and more users interacted with maps, it would become increasingly obvious that the true potential of GIS would come from the users themselves and not the professional data compilers. And as the web turned its focus toward user generated content, the realm of web GIS has come to define the general patterns of online mapping. This introduces a fourth phase to the development of GIS, and leads to a context where mapping has transcended its function as visualization tool and has become a central organizational device for networked communication (Miller, 2006). More specifically, mapping has changed from something that can spatialize social information to something that can socialize spatial information. Once information is geolocated, it becomes the context and content for social interaction.

Net Locality

The Google purchase of the digital mapping service company Keyhole Corp. in 2004 was a major catalyst for the recent shift in mapping practices. Keyhole's database of satellite images could be stitched together so that they seamlessly scrolled and zoomed, effectively transforming static maps into dynamic, malleable documents. And in addition to the vector graphics of the common online map, the satellite images contributed to the sense of seamlessness. The map did not appear to be an individual object, but a fluid rendition of the "state of the earth."

While the fluidity of the Google interface was important, the true innovation didn't emerge from interface designs passed down by the company's employees, but from some very clever hackers. Soon after the launch of Google Maps, users began to appropriate the API to create mashups from existing datasets. Adrian Holovaty, an early Google explorer, overlaid Chicago Police Department crime statistics with a Google map. When the site was active, users were able to search for crimes by type, street, date, police district, zip code, ward, or location. It immediately became popular with homeowners or prospective homebuyers who wanted to determine the safety of neighborhoods.

By July 2005, Google had decided to release its API to anybody who wanted it. As a direct consequence, the web was inundated with Google Maps mashups: everything from personal photos to the best bike paths in town to the content of movies and television shows. That same year, Mike Pegg (2005–2006) started a blog called Google Maps Mania as a means of keeping track of these projects. Currently, the site references thousands of maps, and is updated on a daily basis. The maps are organized into categories such as: current events, transit and transportation, housing and real estate, weather and earth, beer and wine, blogs, TV, movies, celebrities, etc.[2]

So how is this unique from previous phases of GIS? While the web-GIS phase afforded increased access to spatialized data, it did not enable flexibility for the user to choose and produce the dataset. And while it provided some ability to interact with the data, it was not premised on that interaction. In the fourth phase of GIS, maps are not visual documents to be consumed; they are interfaces through which users access, alter and deploy networked data. If the basic functionality of GIS is the integration of databases with maps, where the database is manifested and reflected onto the map, we can begin to understand current practices as a reversal of that reflection. *The map is reflected in the database.* The integration of this fourth phase of GIS into many aspects of web search has altered the general user approach to data.

A Google map is a portal into an expansive database of information. It has options for text search, as well as visual location browsing. For example, a search for "Chicago, IL" retrieves a map, but more importantly, it retrieves an interface from which to conduct further searches. Photographs, You-Tube videos, Wikipedia articles as well as business listings are all represented through "placemarks." Clicking on these placemarks provides direct access to media and external sources through a dialogue window that emerges from the map. While this data could be accessed through the Google text interface, the map provides a geographical clustering that is fundamentally distinct from the textual list. The data is the same, but as users continue to interface with it, the wide expanse of web data becomes increasingly dependent upon the metaphor of physical space and the relative location of the user within that metaphorical space.

Google, and its users' appropriation of its mapping API, have had a substantial influence on transforming mapping from a specialized and deliberate practice to a general and implicit act of navigation. Google Maps, while not the only game in town, has been a game changer. Google has had more to do with normalizing mapping practices than any other company. While this was partly a result of "open sourcing" its map API, it actually had more to do with its efforts to universalize geographic protocols. As a result of the Google acquisition of Keyhole in 2004, the company established the Keyhole Markup Language (KML), which provided a general schema for expressing geographic annotation and visualization for 2D and 3D map interfaces. KML is the geographic version of XML (Extensible Markup Language), which is used to import structured data from one application to another. For example, if someone wanted to move a blog from Blogger to WordPress, they would just need to import the

XML file into the new system. The XML file contains information about formatting, links, and users. Similarly, a KML file includes information about elements such as placemarks, longlat coordinates, images, polygons, and 3D models. It allows someone to transfer a map from two distinct systems – from Google Maps to any other KML enabled system. And it enables Google Maps to crawl through other mapped information to enhance its own search results. In 2008, Google announced that it was "donating" KML, which had been a proprietary protocol, to the Open Geospatial Consortium (OGC). While this move has received extensive praise in the geospatial developer community, the willingness of Google to open source KML was not an act of altruism. It was a push to further naturalize mapping practices, which, in addition to creating more competition, has created more spatialized data that is compatible with the Google spatialized search interface.

When Google first released its API, the initial innovation was in the flexibility of choosing datasets. Users capable of a little coding could take any dataset and plot in onto a map. Within a few years, Google improved its interface to make map creation as easy as clicking a "My Maps" button. With this, the population of single function maps on the web exploded. Maps of public toilets, area codes, restaurants, UFO sightings, or the like were near ubiquitous.[3] At the same time, a number of new platforms launched that sought to take advantage of the multi-functional possibilities of maps. While a Google map can display a single dataset, unless it is purposively restricted, the interface is open to accessing other data as well. Systems such as Platial and Frappr were designed to take advantage of the multi-functional possibilities of mapping.

Platial defines itself as the "people's guide to who and what's near by." Using the Google API, Platial provides an easy way of mapping people and things around specific topics. Fans of Lil' Kim or 50 Cent can find one another with "profiles" and "shout outs" attached to placemarks. Topics ranging from favorite yarn shops to best coffee serve as the premise of connecting users. There are more serious topics as well – from Gulf Coast recovery to local agriculture. The Farm Aid map encourages people in the New York area to plot local farmers. Anyone can join and participate in this map; as long as the map is designated as open by the creator, Platial maps can be viewed either on the Platial website or they can be embedded in blogs, Facebook profiles, or any other mapping application that is KML compatible.

Similarly, Frappr (which was acquired by Platial in 2007) provides comparable functionality, but is designed primarily to be a widget running in other applications. Anyone can create a map, invite other users, and embed it in an existing social network. Both Platial and Frappr are examples of Google Maps mashup systems that prioritize the social networking potential of browsing and visualizing geographic data. They harness the metaphor of physicality to situate users within datasets – the most important of which is the plotted location of other users. For example, a fan site for the popular ABC television series *Lost* hosted a Frappr map so fans could locate each other. Logan, from Iowa City, proudly claimed that he was "Reppin' *Lost* in the Midwest." In this case, the map served to orient the individual user, attached to the community through the common affection of a placeless media object, back to his or her physical location. While the community is still dispersed, fandom is located. Google Maps is being deployed in workplaces and classrooms, professional organizations and fan communities to provide geographical context to a potentially placeless world of networked data. In some cases, this practice might just be a novel use of an online tool while in others it provides a significant layer of context for a community's cohesiveness (Kirschenbaum & Russ, 2002).

Maps have become more than single function tools. Users are increasingly willing to locate themselves within whatever dataset they engage. As an example, let us consider the Facebook Neighborhoods application. Adding this application to a Facebook profile enables users to cluster other users around their designated neighborhood. Users can identify people in their local geographic network. While Neighborhoods does not actually incorporate a map into its interface, it prioritizes the cultural categories of neighborhoods over the objective categories of city perimeters. It requires the individual user to locate themselves within a relative geographical framework for the application to function. As a growth strategy, the application incorporates a competition amongst users to locate other users. By offering "neighborhood builder" points (5 for each invitation and 50 for each accepted invitation), it provides an incentive for participation. The top neighborhood builders, along with their points, are listed along the side of the main screen. The application builds into its local effect organizing strategies similar to community organizing. Being a local organizer within a global network provides possibilities for recognition rarely seen in neighborhood politics.

The incentive to plot oneself in the rapidly expanding network of maps is motivated by the same human connection whose loss the early critics of GIS lamented. But opposed to the criticism levied against earlier versions of GIS, there is now a rhetoric of populism and user-control that was completely absent from previous generations. To map and to be mapped can indeed be empowering, and it is also clearly the commercial goal of several powerful corporations who have a great deal to gain from the increasingly located world (Gordon, 2007; Thompson, 2009). Google has significant interest in making everything locatable; by trying to position its maps as the transparent interface into large data sets, like it did with ascending numerical and alphabetical text search, it can position itself as the gatekeeper, not only to geographic information, but also to geographic knowledge more generally.

Representational maps

Looking at placemarkers on a map is one thing, but zooming into streetscapes is quite another. Google launched its Street View feature in May 2007 – another toggle on the map that lets users zoom into a series of interlocking panoramic photographs. By clicking on direction arrows, users can "walk" down the middle of the street and look around. Street View premiered with coverage of five cities: New York, Las Vegas, San Francisco, Denver, and Miami. Within a little more than a year, coverage expanded to over 80 cities, in some cases including surrounding towns and suburbs as well as national parks and recreation areas. The official company statement is that it intends to cover the entire globe.

The experience of Street View is much more intimate than the top down view provided by satellite images; it enables users to actually see what a building or street looks like. Unlike other features in Google Maps, which aggregate existing datasets into a map interface, Street View requires a bit more direct action from the company. Cars or vans, mounted with cameras, drive around and snap thousands of pictures that are then assimilated into a universal perspective and connected to the map. And more importantly, Street View communicates a feeling of *immersion* within the map. Immersion can be described as a sense of "being there" (Smith *et al.*, 1998). It reduces the perceived distance between located data and the user experiencing the data, and it is likely that future mapping applications will build on this feeling of immersion in order to more strongly map information available on the web to local physical spaces.

This tactic has been so successful that it has spawned a kind of online tourism. When Street View was first launched, several "tourist" sites emerged devoted to featuring noteworthy photographs. *Wired News* started a competition for its readers to identify interesting pictures – starting in San Francisco and New York, and later in Los Angeles and San Diego. The results were fascinating: a man seemingly breaking into a building in San Francisco, car accidents in Minneapolis, Phoenix, and Oceanside, California, a man lasciviously eyeing a woman stretching in San

Figure 1.2 Google Street View image of a stuffed animal house on Mount Elliot and Elba Place, Detroit, Michigan. © 2010 Google.

Francisco, a stuffed animal house in Detroit, and a man being arrested in St Louis. Most of these images are mere curiosities, but some have sparked considerable controversy, raising serious issues about privacy and surveillance, which we will address more thoroughly in Chapter 6.

These touristic practices bring some important issues to the foreground. As localities become networked, maps serve as representations of those networks (this is in addition to their function as tools). Street View allows a user to explore new localities, not simply to facilitate interactions with existing ones. While exploration has been a popular use of maps for centuries, the map has before only facilitated physical exploration. Now, the map becomes a location that is, itself, worthy of exploring.

On the surface, this is reminiscent of what the postmodern theorist Jean Baudrillard said of the effects of simulation on the "real" world. He forcefully stated that the "territory no longer precedes the map, the map now precedes the territory" (Baudrillard, 1994, p. 1). Speaking metaphorically about representations in contemporary culture, he suggested that representations have become more "real" than the things they represent – a phenomenon he dubbed the simulacrum. According to Baudrillard, the tourist photograph would drive the experience of the tourist destination and not the other way around. However, it is clear that within net locality an online destination in itself does not replace the thing it maps. Rather, it makes the connection to that physical location even stronger. As we will see in the next chapter, digital information can actually become part of the physical location, instead of destroying, or replacing it. The map itself is desirable, but only because it maps the world of information into the world.

This becomes strikingly clear when looking at the 3D mapping features present in Bing and Google Earth. Building on the immersive qualities of Street View, tools like Google Earth or 3D Bird's Eye street view in Bing Maps add camera effects that bring the user even closer to the map. When launching Google Earth as a standalone application or as a web plug-in, the camera zooms down from a picture of the whole Earth to 3D models of streetscapes placed atop high-resolution satellite imagery.

Within Google Earth, users can access and add information, videos and photos – but they can also access and add 3D models of buildings using the Google SketchUp application.[4] Any model built with SketchUp can be placed in one's personal map view; and if it is really good, it can be sent to the Google "model warehouse" where it can be selected to become part of the "official record." Hundreds of cities throughout the world have already been modeled in this way, and new cities are constantly coming online, facilitated by the "cities in development" program on the Google Earth website. With at least 12 models correctly built and georeferenced, modelers can create calls for other contributors. Google boasts over 500,000 registered users that are actively adding content, whether models, photos, or placemarks, to the rapidly expanding database of the online globe.

Some cities and towns have started using these models to assist in the community planning process. Amherst, Massachusetts, for instance, commissioned the building of the town center in 2007 as part of their master planning process. The models were uploaded to the 3D warehouse and have since become part of the Google Earth landscape. The city of Amherst has used the 3D models in various ways – to show communities what future developments might like look or to facilitate city tours. "This is exactly what we were hoping to accomplish," says Niels la Cour, who spearheaded and launched the Amherst in 3D project when he was senior planner for the town, "This is a way to enable people to envision economic development that's about what they really want, versus something like a strip mall."[5]

Other towns have embarked on similar efforts: McMinnville Tennessee, in partnership with Google, built a 3D model of the downtown primarily as

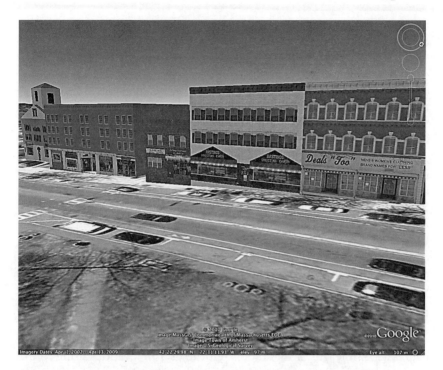

Figure 1.3 View of Amherst, Massachusetts in Google Earth. © 2010 Google.

a means of encouraging development. Chris Wilson, the executive director of Main Street McMinnville, says that people are excited by this project because

> they can put together a persuasive presentation to sell their idea for a business or industry – right out of the box. You could find a lot in McMinnville, build a 3D model, and show exactly what the customer will see walking down the street. It's a way to show that you "did your homework" – you understand the dynamics of making a business successful in a small town.[6]

As tools and methods of production become more efficient, the purview of the mappable world expands. Google has even ventured into mapping the stars and the oceans, and others have attempted to map interiors. The livable, and therefore mappable, world extends beyond building facades. EveryScape is an interesting example of this. It is devoted to mapping interiors. While Google and Microsoft have been able to deploy cars with cameras mounted to their roofs around streets in hundreds of cities, it would be impractical and illegal for them to photograph the insides of buildings. So, they have set out to crowdsource this process. They contract citizen cartographers to photograph city streets and interiors. Their strategy is quite clear – they align Google with Big Brother by emphasizing their own reliance on user-generated content. EveryScape provides the necessary camera equipment and car mounts and pays by the mile for "ambassadors" to produce panoramic images. They also integrate content from Flickr, Yelp, and YouTube into the images themselves, and make it possible for users to share memos on specific locations with others. It has an internal advertising mechanism, where businesses can place ads on the street or can include an interior view of their establishment. Harvard Square in Cambridge, Massachusetts, one of the EveryScape pilot neighborhoods, has 25 interiors that can be explored in a single square mile shopping district. As users browse through "the world online," they can read digital billboards or stumble into restaurants and pubs. This is the feature that the company hopes will allow it to compete with Google. "I'm quite confident," EveryScape CEO Jim Schoonmaker told the *Boston Globe*, "that if we have world coverage of interiors and exteriors, people will leave Google and come to us" (Bray, 2008).

These new types of maps are representations of net localities, where the experience of *being there* is the experience of being in a location where data is accessible. All of these tools put the user in locations using formal visual elements like camera zoom and pan, but the real depth of the immersion comes from the fact that the user is surrounded by pictures, comments, models and anything else that can be tied to that specific location. They communicate the user's presence in a location, but, more importantly, they communicate the location's presence with the user. With locations always present, these maps can empower the user to see in new ways.

Is the World Too Much With Us?

Maps enable us to make sense of information that is located in the world. Because of the near ubiquity of maps, we are often acting in service to them. We are going out of our way to locate things: putting geo-coordinates on a Flickr photo, identifying a neighborhood on Facebook, mapping the location of individuals in fan groups or professional organizations. We believe it is in our best interests to service the map. But like most things involving user-generated content, these practices are both empowering and potentially disempowering. As Trebor Scholz (2008) argues about the web more generally, just as these tools promise greater personal control of our networked surroundings, they also promise external financial and political interests greater control over us. Just as we map ourselves to map others, we offer ourselves up to be mapped by others. Just as we gain control of the mappable world, we lose control with the realization that we are part of the world to be mapped.

In William Wordsworth's famous 1807 sonnet, he warns that "the world is too much with us." In this early nineteenth century perspective, the materialist world born of capitalism has removed us from the wonders of nature, making us incapable of seeing what is right in front of our eyes. We lose the world because we believe we are capable of controlling it. It is not difficult to see the connection between Wordsworth's powerful words and the implications of net localities. The more we have the map to orient our place in the world, the less comfortable we are with not having it. The world is, indeed, with us. But, is it too much with us? The map creates our world; it does not simply mediate it. It has so thoroughly saturated our culture that it would be fruitless to even contemplate extracting the map from the mapped. Moving forward, we need to understand the systems we have created and how best to navigate them.

Notes

1 Notable criticisms include Harris & Weiner, 1996; McHaffie, 1995; and Pickles, 1995.
2 In June 2008, Mike Pegg stepped down from the reigns of Google Maps Mania to take a full time job at Google on their geo-marketing team.
3 See http://safe2pee.org/beta, http://www.usnaviguide.com/areacode.htm, www.toeat.com, www.ufomaps.com, respectively, all retrieved November 1, 2010.
4 Google has released a free version and a pro version to enhance its market penetration.
5 See http://sketchup.google.com/3dwh/citiesin3d/amherst.html, retrieved November 1, 2010.
6 See http://sketchup.google.com/3dwh/citiesin3d/mcminnville.html, retrieved November 1, 2010.

References

Agüerra y Arcas, B. (2010, February). Blaise Agüera y Arcas demos augmented-reality maps [Video]. *TED Talks*. Retrieved November 1, 2010 from http://www.ted.com/talks/blaise_aguera.html

Baudrillard, J. (1994). *Simulacra and simulation*. Ann Arbor: University of Michigan Press.

Bray, H. (2008, June 24). Take a peek: EveryScape plans to put interiors on the map. *The Boston Globe*, p. C1.

Butler, D. (2006). The web wide world. *Nature*, *439*(16), 776–778.

Clark, M. (1998). GIS – democracy or delusion? *Environment and Planning A*, *30*, 303–316.

Eisentein, E. (1979). *The printing press as an agent of change: Communications and cultural transformations in early modern Europe*. New York: Cambridge University Press.

Foresman, T. W. (1998). GIS early years and the threads of evolution. In Foresman, T. W. (Ed.), *The history of Geographic Information Systems* (pp. 3–17). Upper Saddle River, NJ: Prentice Hall.

Goodchild, M.F. (2007). Citizens as voluntary sensors: Spatial data infrastructure in the world of Web 2.0. *International Journal of Spatial Data Infrastructures Research*, *2*, 24–32.

Gordon, E. (2007). Mapping digital networks: From cyberspace to Google. *Information, Communication and Society*, *10*(6), 885–901.

Haklay, M., Singleton, A., & Parker, C. (2008). Web mapping 2.0: The neo-geography of the GeoWeb. *Geography Compass*, *2*(6), 2011–2039.

Harder, C. (1998). *Serving maps on the Internet: Geographic information on the World Wide Web*. Redlands, CA: Environmental Systems Research Institute, Inc.

Harris, T., & Weiner, D. (1996). *GIS and society: The social implications of how people, space, and environment are represented in GIS*. Santa Barbara, CA: NCGIA Technical Report.

Kirschenbaum, J., & Russ, L. (2002). *Community mapping: Using geographic data for neighborhood revitalization*. Oakland, CA: PolicyLink.

Kohn, C. M. (1970). The 1960s: A decade of progress in geographical research and instruction. *Annals of the Association of American Geographers*, *60*, 211–219.

Malczewski, J. (2004). GIS-based land-use suitability analysis: A critical overview. *Progress in Planning*, *62*, 3–65.

McHaffie, P. H. (1995). Manufacturing metaphors: Public cartography, the market, and democracy. In Pickles, J. (Ed.), *Ground truth: The social implications of Geographic Information Systems*, (pp. 113–129). New York: Guilford Press.

Merril, R., & Timmreck, T. (2006). *Introduction to epidemiology*. Boston, MA: Jones & Bartlett.

Miller, C. C. (2006). A beast in the field: The Google Maps mashup as GIS/2. *Cartographia*, *41*, 187–199.

Pegg, M. (2005–2006). *Google Maps Mania: An unofficial Google Maps blog tracking the websites, mashups and tools being influenced by Google Maps*. Retrieved November 1, 2010 from http://googlemapsmania.blogspot.com/

Peng, Z. R., & Tsou, M. H. (2003). *Internet GIS: Distributed Geographic Information Services for the internet and wireless network*. Hoboken, NJ: John Wiley & Sons, Inc.

Peterson, M. (1999). Trends in internet map use: A Second Look. *Proceedings of the 19th International Cartographic Conference*. Ottawa, Canada.

Pickles, J. (1995). Representations in an electronic age: Geography, GIS, and democracy. In Pickles, J. (Ed.), *Ground truth: The social implications of Geographic Information Systems* (pp. 1–30). New York: Guilford Press.

Ptolemy, C. (1991). *The geography.* New York: Dover.

Scharl, A., & Tochtermann, K. (Eds.). (2007). *The Geospatial Web: How geobrowsers, social software and the Web 2.0 are shaping the network society.* London: Springer.

Scholz, T. (2008). Market ideology and the myths of Web 2.0. *First Monday, 13*(3). Retrieved November 1, 2010 from http://firstmonday.org/htbin/cgiwrap/bin/ojs/index.php/fm/article/view/2138/1945

Smith, S., Marsh, T., Duke, D., & Wright, P. (1998). Drowning in immersion. *Proceedings from UK-VRSIG '98: The Fifth Conference of the UK Virtual Reality Special Interest Group* (pp. 1–9). Exeter, UK.

Thompson, C. (2009, June 31). *Future of the web: Location, location, location.* Retrieved November 1 2010 from http://www.wired.com/dualperspectives/article/news/2009/06/dp_web_wired0630

Tomlinson, R. (1998). The Canada geographic information system. In Foresman, T. W. (Ed.), *The history of geographic information systems* (pp. 21–32). Upper Saddle River, NJ: Prentice Hall.

Tufte, E. (1997). *Visual explanations: Images and quantities, evidence and narrative.* Cheshire, CT: Graphics Press.

Turner, A. (2006). *Introduction to neogeography* [PDF version]. Retrieved November 1, 2010 from http://oreilly.com/catalog/9780596529956/

Wright, J. K. (1936). A method of mapping densities of population: With Cape Cod as an example. *Geographical Review, 26*(1), 103–110.

Wright, J. K. (1947). Terrae Incognitae: The place of the imagination in geography. *Annals of the Association of American Geographers, 37*, 1–15. Retrieved November 1, 2010 from http://www.colorado.edu/geography/giw/wright-jk/1947_ti/body.html

2

Mobile Annotations

Mobile phones enable us to stay connected to each other, even when we are away from the home or office. We can be nearly anywhere and pick up the phone to make a call. We no longer need to coordinate with other people before going someplace, because regardless of where it is, we can just "call when we get there." Sociologist Barry Wellman (2001) has suggested that "mobile phones afford a fundamental liberation from place, and they soon will be joined by wireless computers and personalized software" (p. 238). Similarly, Hans Geser (2004) has noted that the mobile phone frees people from spatial fixity. Of course, this freedom has a dark side as well. With no implicit connection to physical location, widespread use of the mobile phone could send us spiraling into a placeless world without regard to location. Tsugio Makimoto and David Manners (1997) argue that people who use digital mobile technologies have the ability to walk around connected, making them "geographically independent" (p. 2).

However, precisely *because* mobile phones are not "attached" to specific places, conversations require spatial contextualization. It is a common refrain in mobile phone conversations to ask "Where are you?" (Laurier, 2001). We want to be aware of location, because physicality provides an important cognitive grounding for communication. It helps to visualize what is on the other end of a conversation. Location mattered even in the beginning when mobile phones were used mostly as, well, mobile telephones. Back when they were merely two-way voice communication devices, people could only talk about location because the devices had no way of knowing where they were. Even when triangulation of radio

Net Locality: Why Location Matters in a Networked World, First Edition. Eric Gordon and Adriana de Souza e Silva. © 2011 Eric Gordon and Adriana de Souza e Silva. Published 2011 by Blackwell Publishing Ltd.

waves could be used to detect a device's location, the information was typically not accessible to users.

While of course many people in the world still use phones of this sort, mobile "phones" equipped with web connectivity, location awareness, and operating systems (aka "smart phones") are the fastest growing market segment. Almost all "smart" phones today are location aware. They typically have a Global Positioning System (GPS) receiver and corresponding software so that users can pinpoint their location on a map. When phones are location aware, location can be more than just a mere curiosity or grounding metaphor: it can be a tool for navigating information. A myriad of applications have been built to facilitate this kind of navigation, such as those that allow users to find nearby restaurants and gas stations, and social networks, which allow users to find other people in their surroundings. While location-aware mobile applications are a relatively new phenomenon (most of them became popular around 2008, after the release of the iPhone 3G), there is an important history that informed the development of location-aware mobile phones. They were not invented by Apple or Research In Motion (the company that makes Blackberry devices); they emerged out of experimentation and exploration of our very real desire to locate and be located. All of the experiments we will discuss in this chapter have contributed to the ecosystem of location-based applications that enable what we now call net locality.

Locating Devices

By being able to connect to satellites, mobile phone towers, or wireless routers, mobile devices acquire geospatial coordinates that allow users to access information about their location and to find other users in the area. Location awareness in mobile phones can be accomplished in three ways: cellular triangulation, the Global Positioning System (GPS), and/or Wi-Fi positioning. Cellular triangulation indicates the device's location through the triangulation of radio waves detected by the mobile phone's location in relation to transmission towers. It is not very precise, but it is a feature of every mobile phone. Since 2002, the Federal Communications Commission (FCC) has required that all wireless carriers are able to locate subscribers' mobile phones when dialing 911. GPS devices indicate the exact location of the device on Earth with a small margin of error through a constellation of satellites. Although GPS technology has existed since the early 1960s, it was not until the Clinton Administration removed the signal degradation called Select Availability (SA) on May 1, 2000 that these devices became popular. After that, GPS devices, previously only available to the American military and government, became much more accurate, allowing users to locate specific places and objects on the globe's surface.

In March 2003, NTT DOCOMO, the main Japanese mobile phone provider, announced the first GPS mobile phone in Japan (NTT DOCOMO, 2003), which allowed mobile phone users to find directions, look for nearby restaurants, and find out when the next bus was coming. In the United States, it was just in 2008, with the release of the GPS-enabled iPhone 3G and the Google Android system, that location-based applications started to become popular. Recently, Wi-Fi technologies have also been used by companies such as Skyhook Wireless to complement cellular triangulation and GPS in the task of locating a mobile phone. Because cellular triangulation is not very precise and GPS sometimes does not work (for example, while indoors or on a cloudy day GPS signals might be weak or nonexistent), Skyhook created a location system in which mobile phones might transition across all three technologies, depending on which one is available. Furthermore, if more than one technology is available, for example Wi-Fi and cellular triangulation, the system uses hybrid positioning, which determines the location of mobile devices with much more accuracy: about 10–20 meters (Kirsner, 2005). Since 2003, Skyhook has employed drivers to map Wi-Fi access points in major US, Asian, and European cities. With more and more mobile devices becoming location aware in one way or another, location-based applications have proliferated.

Attaching Information to Location

As early as 1996, Jim Spohrer (1999) envisioned a system called World-Board, which would use technology to augment physical space with digital information. Using GPS devices, WorldBoard allowed information to be attached to specific places, by superimposing digital data on the concrete physical world. As Spohrer (1999) said, "Imagine being able to enter an airport and see a virtual red carpet leading you right to your gate, look at the ground and see property lines or underground buried cables, walk along a nature trail and see virtual signs near plants and rocks, or simply look at the night sky and see the outlines of the constellations" (p. 602).

Spohrer foresaw three types of display technologies through which users could access localized digital information "attached" to the physical world: head-mounted see-through display glasses, hand held palm-sized devices, and projectors that could superimpose images on the environment. Head-mounted displays (HMD) attracted a substantial amount of attention during the 1990s, especially with the unfulfilled expectation that the web would primarily be accessed as an immersive 3D virtual world. During this time, many artists developed virtual reality environments. Some examples are Char Davies' *Osmose* (1995) and *Ephémère* (1998), and Brenda Laurel and Rachel Strickland's *Placeholder* (1992), which required users to wear an HMD as an interface to interact with the environment. Sci-fi movies and novels such as *Johnny Mnemonic* (Longo, 1995) and *The Thirteenth Floor* (Rusnak, 1999) also portrayed types of HMD as interfaces to connect to virtual worlds and the web. In the first decade of the twenty-first century, however, most display technologies used to access or show digital data are projection and portable devices.

As Spohrer noted, hand held technologies were easier to carry and store than HMDs: they produced no nausea effects, and they allowed more than one person to look at the information display at the same time, creating a sort of social environment. Similarly, projections on urban spaces might also promote social interaction and communication (Spohrer, 1999, p. 609). An early example of large projection screens that reconfigured the social urban dynamics of both New York and Los Angeles is Kit Galloway and Sherrie Rabinowitz's art installation *Hole in Space* (1980).[1] In this pioneering use of satellite technology, the artists placed a life-sized screen showing live images of the streets of New York in Los Angeles and vice versa. Without previous warnings or signs, people in each city paused in front of the screens and began chatting with their remote counterparts. The video documentation of the piece during three consecutive days shows that initially the public was mesmerized by the possibility of live interaction with the other city, often doubting that the people on the other side were actually there. On the second and third days, however, people realized the strong social potential of the piece, and started scheduling meetings in order to get in touch with friends and family members whom they hadn't seen for years. By trying to redefine "image as a place," the artists managed to create an unexpected feeling of remote co-presence, which is common today with the use of videoconferencing technology. The innovation of *Hole in Space*, however, was not solely its ability to project a remote live image via satellite – it was the placement of the projection screen in a busy public urban space, leading to unexpected reactions from the public, and feelings of connections and disconnections to location.

The screens in *Hole in Space* were physically attached to locations, but the piece paved the way to a future where images and information could be *digitally* attached to physical locations. Furthermore, by foregrounding the mix of local and remote social connections enabled by the public screens,

Figure 2.1 Kit Galloway and Sherrie Rabinowitz's *Hole in Space* (1980). Reproduced by permission of Kit Galloway and Sherrie Rabinowitz.

Hole in Space foresaw the impact that information attached to locations would have on local social interactions.

Spohrer anticipated the development of net locality. He understood that the desire for location was going to dictate the technologies that delivered it. He suggested three ways in which physical locations ("places," in his terminology) could be transformed by the use of location-aware technologies. First, non-physical information can exist in a physical space. Information overlaid on physical space becomes part of the space, not just an augmentation of it. Second, the same location can appear differently according to who perceives it and for what purpose. Depending on the available technology (or lack thereof), people might be able to experience urban spaces in different ways. Finally, many of the most useful properties of a location, such as its history, can be stored with it, perhaps altering the need for going home to look for information in an encyclopedia or on the web from a desktop computer. Even in 1999, he understood the need for information and locations to merge. And his ideas have proven very influential for many of the early experiments in producing and occupying net localities.

Tracing and Mapping Locations

Spohrer's WorldBoard was never implemented, and the development of works that experimented with location-aware technologies did not really start until the beginning of the 2000s. When most people were still thinking of mobile phones as mobile landlines, locative media artists were already trying to figure out what happens when people used their phones not only to talk to remote people, but also to engage with digitally located information and the physical space around them. Many of the early projects developed by locative media artists predate location-aware smart phones and, as a result, typically employed stand-alone GPS devices as their main technology. They included some kind of tracing and mapping, using the GPS device to track movements (of people and things) through physical space. Some well-known examples are Jeremy Wood's *GPS Drawing* (2000), Teri Rueb's *The Choreography of Everyday Movement* (2001), the Waag Society's *Amsterdam Real Time* (2002), and Esther Polak and Leva Auzina's *MILKproject* (2004). Rueb's piece, for example, was an art installation that tracked participant's movements through the city with a GPS device. Their trajectories were then transformed into drawings and printed onto acetate, registered against prior journeys, and sandwiched between stacked plates of glass that were then displayed in a gallery. By collecting snapshots of people's movement through space and time, *The Choreography of Everyday Movement* allowed museum visitors to literally visualize the paths that people take in urban spaces.

Rueb's project froze participants' trajectories and collected them for later visualization, but the Waag Society's *Amsterdam Real Time* installation tracked participants in real time, so that their mobility through downtown Amsterdam could be sent live to the exhibition *Maps of Amsterdam 1866–2000* in which the project was being displayed. In doing so, the piece forced visitors to contrast the traditional maps of the city with the digital maps plotted with the mobility of people. *Amsterdam Real Time* was a collectively constructed GIS map; that is, it was built by tracing the movement of people through space. This project made clear the value in producing maps through real-time social participation. It sought to make people more aware of the physical spaces around them by giving them the tools to analyze real-time social patterns. These early mapping projects in locative media art aimed at something similar to the maps we discussed in Chapter 1. The maps in these pieces did not pre-exist the artwork. Rather, they were constructed through the participants' contributions and experiences of physical space. As a result, they could be transformative of the user's experiences of urban spaces.

While some projects got users to trace their personal movement to create new patterns, others sought to have users trace existing patterns with their movement. These were often called "walks" – or audio tours triggered by the location of the user. Audio walks were developed by many artists, such as Janet Cardiff's *Her Long Black Hair* (2004–2005), Jeff Knowlton, Jeremy Hight, and Naomi Spellman's *34 North 118 West* (2002) and

Figure 2.2 Waag Society with Esther Polak and Jeroen Kee, *Amsterdam Real-Time* (2002). © 2002 Waag Society/Esther Polak. Reproduced by permission of the Waag Society.

Teri Rueb's *Itinerant* (2005). Janet Cardiff was the first artist to become famous for audio walks. Cardiff's initial projects did not include any location-aware technology. They simply overlaid a fictitious narrative over a familiar urban space by creating guided tours to which participants could listen. They were directed through a specific location by following instructions like "walk two blocks, then turn left." The goal of Cardiff's projects was to make participants aware of their physical location. But technological limitations curtailed their effectiveness. Because the location of the user was not automatically detected, the success of the piece depended on the user correctly following the instructions given by the artist. If a participant took a wrong turn, the experience would be lost. Automated GPS positioning changed this scenario. One of the first

Figure 2.3 Jeff Knowlton, Jeremy Hight, and Naomi Spellman's *34 North 118 West* (2002). Reproduced by permission of Jeremy Hight.

GPS-enabled audio walks was Knowlton, Hight, and Spellman's *34 North 118 West*. Named after the geographical coordinates of the city of Los Angeles, the project invited participants to uncover narratives about Los Angeles' history as they navigated through the city's downtown. Equipped with GPS-enabled Tablet PCs and headphones, participants heard stories about the places they were moving through, triggered by their location.

More recently, Teri Rueb developed *Itinerant*, an interactive sound installation in downtown Boston. Equipped with a pair of headphones connected to a small Pocket PC with GPS and custom software, participants experienced a story that reframed Mary Shelley's Frankenstein in the streets of Boston. "The participant's movement, tracked by the GPS, triggers the playback of the sounds as she moves through parts of the city space where sounds have been 'placed'" (Rueb, 2007, p. 273). These installations created an audio layer on top of the city space, with the intention of making users experience familiar urban spaces in unfamiliar ways. Audio walks were one of the first attempts to digitally attach information to locations. However, although audio walks could be experienced in groups, as is the case in the picture below, participants could not change or share the information they encountered. That is, until "geotagging," or mobile annotation, was added to the toolkit.

Mobile Annotation

The first mobile annotation projects are ones that took literally Spohrer's framework. In addition to media artists, researchers and scholars were also interested in exploring the ability of attaching information to locations. GeoNotes, developed in 2000 by the Swedish Institute of Computer Science, detected the geographical position of the user's PC or personal digital assistant (PDA) via Wi-Fi, allowing them to digitally produce "tags" and "graffiti" in their location (Persson, Espinoza, & Cacciatore, 2001). Other users of the system could access these virtual notes when in the vicinity. GeoNotes, however, was an indoor application; it only worked within the domain of the wireless local area network (LAN) inside a building, so there was no implication for the experience of urban spaces, as with the other projects we have been describing.

This changed in 2002, when UK-based art group Proboscis developed the project *Urban Tapestries* (2002–2004) to investigate "how the combination of GIS and mobile technologies could enable people to map and share their knowledge and experience, stories and information" (Proboscis, 2002–2004), creating what they called "public authoring." Distinct from the GPS audio walks, where users followed a narrative created by the artists, *Urban Tapestries* allowed participants to attach geographical coordinates to stories, pictures, sounds, and video and upload them to a server, embedding social knowledge into the fabric of the city. This digital information could then be retrieved when another user was near the location of the information. *Urban Tapestries* enabled participants to become authors and co-creators of their digital/physical environments.

Digital annotation with mobile devices did not need to employ GPS to attach information to locations. *Yellow Arrow* (2004), for example, was a project aimed at creating a new way of exploring cities by actually inverting the traditional geotagging experience. *Yellow Arrow* was conceived by Counts Media, a New York-based gaming company, in 2004 as a MAAP (Massively Authored Artistic Publication) of the world. The premise was simple. Users would order yellow arrow stickers and shirts from the website, each marked with a unique code, and place or wear them throughout the city. Once placed or worn, users would send an SMS or access the website to annotate the unique code of the sticker or shirt. Once annotated, the message associated with the code can be changed as often as the user likes. So when a user comes across a yellow arrow in the city, they

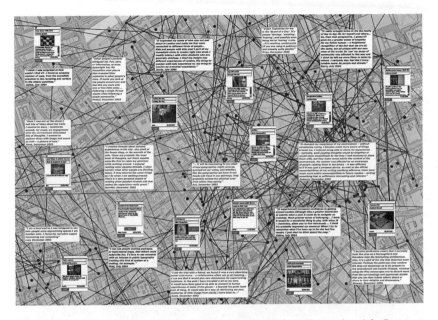

Figure 2.4 A map of threads created during the *Urban Tapestries* trial. Contexts Map, *Urban Tapestries* (2002–2004) by Proboscis, http://proboscis.org.uk. Reproduced by permission of Proboscis.

need only call the number on the arrow and dial the unique code to access the annotation.

Organizations and educators were quick to adopt *Yellow Arrow* to produce alternative narratives of familiar cities. *Connecting Berlin*, sponsored by ITB Berlin, was a four-day festival wherein participants placed arrows throughout Berlin to identify that city's connection to other global cities. One user placed an arrow on a faux Greek column in a food court and wrote: "The Parthenon emerges in Berlin. Is this a stolen Greek treasure like the Elgin marbles or the future of travel?" The question was placed amongst hundreds of others, marked by yellow arrows throughout the city and annotated on the web. *Connecting Berlin* or any of the other dozens of "journeys," afforded users the ability to print out a map of annotations or simply browse online to create a physical or virtual walking tour of the city. Projects like *Urban Tapestries* and *Yellow Arrow* pioneered the development of commercial mobile annotation applications, such as Digital Graffiti and Mscape, discussed below.

While artists set the stage for exploring net localities, corporate and academic researchers were quick to join the fray. There were important

Figure 2.5 Collage of *Yellow Arrow* stickers in cities throughout the world. Photographs courtesy of *Yellow Arrow*. Select arrows placed by bigdad, cook, fortuna, house, jshapes, matta, panda, ph.d, sirHC, sixten, Stemme, Stinky, tourist, urbsmrai, Vid, Vinal, and zoetrope. Reproduced by permission of Jesse Shapins.

questions to be answered and potential profits to be made in configuring usability in the convergence of the web and physical space. In 2005, Siemens, in cooperation with researchers at the University of Linz in Austria and the Ars Electronica Center built on the ideas of previous projects when they announced the development of a project called Digital Graffiti. Instead of going to the web to annotate yellow arrows, Digital Graffiti enabled users to send a text message to any geographic location. Up until then, an SMS was generally sent to another mobile phone user, but with Digital Graffiti, if a user were to send an SMS to a target location, then any other user who subscribed to the service would have the message displayed on his or her screen upon entering that location. Two possible applications for this technology envisioned by Siemens were outdoor tourism guides, by which tourists could read information about monuments and history when approaching specific places, and location-based advertising by which stores could send promotion coupons for people nearby who subscribed to the "advertising mode."

In 2007, soon after Digital Graffiti, Hewlett Packard announced Mscape. It was an authoring toolkit built on Siemens's idea, which enabled people to attach information to places, creating what they called a "mediascape." These included text messages, but also sounds, interactive games, walks, and textures. To create a mediascape, users combined sounds, texts, and images on their computers using special software. The software displayed an online map, where people could attach information to specific places by inputting geographical coordinates. In order to experience mediascapes, users downloaded them to their mobile devices, then went to the physical location for which the mediascape was created. The media would be triggered by the user's geographical location. An example of an interactive mediascape was a game that took place in the Tower of London. The game, built on the model of an audio walk, enabled players to follow a narrative about the tower. To interact with the mediascape users were prompted to tap on a picture of a prisoner. They were then given instructions about where to go and what to find. Their device displayed a map which showed their current position and where they needed to go (Hewlett-Packard Development Company, LP, 2007). The difference between a mediascape and an audio walk is that instead of following a pre-created narrative by the artist, mediascape users were charged with being the authors of their own narratives.

All these mobile annotation applications allowed for the layering of information on location, something already predicted by Spohrer more than a decade earlier. But these locative media projects remained in the experimental domains of art and research until recently. The release of the GPS-enabled iPhone 3G in 2008 and the Google Android system sparked a surge in their popularity, making them available to more people and opening up a myriad of contexts for their use. But, of course, the simple availability of hardware is not the only reason for the popularity of these services. As with every new technology, there are many social, economic, cultural, and technological issues that contribute to their development and adoption (Kellerman, 2006). The cultural currency of net locality more generally has had a large role to play in the availability of these new tools. And the commercial availability of these platforms has further sped up location's transition to the mainstream.

Location Awareness Goes Mainstream

Artists and for-profit companies typically have different motivations: generally speaking, artists subvert established practices and for-profit companies monetize them. Artists have generally tried to challenge accepted interpretations and uses of space, and for profit companies have sought to commodify space. Business models emerge on the premise that information space is available advertising space.

That there is correlation between these practices might strike some as surprising. In the case of locative media, the artists' perspective and the business model have frequently merged. Media art critics Marc Tuters and Kazys Varnelis (2006) note that "where net art sought to maintain its autonomy from the commercial web in order to claim art status, locative media ... has been welcomed with often remarkable claims, in particular by the computer industry" (p. 358). Tuters and Varnelis emphasize the influence of locative media on the development of the geospatial web, by very early on embracing the possibility of art projects intersecting with industry and local governments. Some well-known examples include the group Proboscis, who received sponsorship from telecommunication companies for their piece *Urban Tapestries*, and Blast Theory, whose most prominent pieces have been supported by corporate sponsorship. Still, some have criticized this hybrid art/industry model as ineffective (Galloway, 2005), and others have simply accused it of being apolitical (Broeckmann, 2004, as cited in Tuters & Varnelis, 2006). But whatever the criticism, the way in which these projects have embraced consumer technologies has set the groundwork for similar applications to reach a mass audience.

One of the first examples of a commercial mobile annotation application was WikiMe. WikiMe aggregated Wikipedia entries based on a user's location. Using a mobile phone, the user was presented with several ways of finding Wikipedia information. In one view, she could read a list of entries ordered by their relative distance to her with a brief name and picture of the location, along with the first sentence or two of the Wikipedia entry. Closer entries were listed first. Once the user clicked on a Wikipedia entry, she could also select to see a map view or a photo view of that entry. In the map view, she could see the location of the entry in relation to other entries. In photo view, she could see a list of photos taken near her present location. As with any wiki, users could alter the Wikipedia articles or write new ones. But in the case of WikiMe, they could do so with their mobile device. This is what enables the experience of net locality. Rather than being disconnected from the location the article references, making a change to an article alters the available information about that space, and therefore influences how the user perceives it. There is potential that these changes might influence how other users experience the space. Any change to a Wikipedia article, whether made in the space or remotely, effectively alters the available information landscape for those in the physical location (de Souza e Silva & Sutko, in press).

Other types of mobile geotagging applications developed later were not restricted to Wikipedia articles, but rather aggregated general news stories, discussion threads, blog posts, and tweets relevant to the user's physical location. For example, the Radar service of Outside.in lets iPhone users switch between different scales to find news within 1000 feet of their current location, or stories from the surrounding neighborhood. As with WikiMe, users can choose between a list and a map interface. Similarly, Fwix ties news and media updates to particular locations in a city, showing where media "hotspots" are located.

There is nothing particularly special about any one of these applications. But together they point to a significant trend in using mobile phones as urban annotation tools. Mobile phones have become writing utensils for net localities. They facilitate interactions and cultivate a richness to the maps and spaces in which we are constantly engaged. The specific nature of these applications will certainly change with time. But, in looking at the history of these tools in art and research, there is a consistency to their

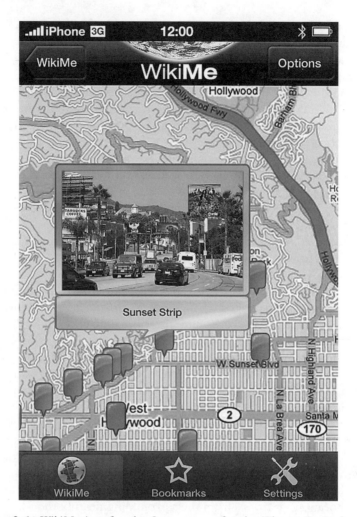

Figure 2.6 WikiMe interface by Supportware for the iPhone. Reproduced by permission of Supportware.

functionality. Mobile annotation applications have enabled us to locate things and to be located ourselves, and the availability of GPS and the affordability of mobile devices have fueled the popular adoption of these tools. Now that our devices our location aware, we are much better positioned to be location aware ourselves.

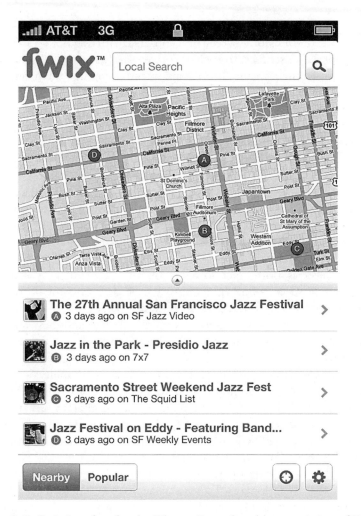

Figure 2.7 Fwix interface for the iPhone. Reproduced by permission of Fwix/ Darian Shiray.

Location is Everywhere

Increasingly, the ability to locate — things, people, information — is becoming a common feature of all mobile software. Roughly a year after the release of the iPhone 3G, almost all iPhone applications started asking users to disclose their location information when downloaded, even if its use was not immediately apparent. In February 2008, Apple filed a patent for "Transitional Data Sets," which described a system that customized the iPhone home screen in accordance with the user's location. So, for example, if a user flies from New York to San Francisco, at the moment he gets out of the airplane, his iPhone would recognize the location and automatically rearrange the application icons on the home screen according to what is perceived useful for that location, such as local weather, time, maps, and contacts (Hughes, 2009).

Mobile applications are becoming context aware, that is, they are aware of the environment and react according to the user's algorithmically determined needs. These developments are becoming faster with the introduction of 4G cellular networks, as we will discuss later. But a question we might ask ourselves at this point is, does the device's location awareness contribute to an increase in the awareness of our physical surroundings? Or, are these applications being developed because we are already more aware of them?

The answer is both. Net locality connotes a context in which our perception of space is influenced both by the development of new technologies and also by our desire to be location aware. As we have seen throughout this chapter, location-aware mobile technologies can change the way we experience both physical and digital spaces by configuring a new hybrid space, which is composed by a mix of digital information and physical localities. As Spohrer noted more than a decade ago, the ability of attaching information to places reconfigures the traditional notion of location. Rather than locations being simply augmented with digital information, net localities emerge as a byproduct of the use of location-aware technologies. They are social spaces filled with digital information – but they are even more interesting than that. Net localities include remote users as well. Users connected to each other and to localities via mobile devices are altering the conditions of physical spaces. To be local means to be engaged with the local conditions of a physical space, whether the user is physically proximate or not. This is a remarkable shift in how we understand urban space and one that becomes more remarkable when we confront the issue of co-presence. In net localities, being someplace is determined by physical and digital proximity. How this happens is the topic of the next chapter.

Notes

1   Recent examples of projects that use projection technologies to change the experience of the urban landscape are the works of Rafael Lozano-Hemmer (series of relational architectures) and the Chaos Computer Club's *Blinkenlights* (2001).

References

Broeckmann, A. (2004). *Exhibiting locative media: CRUMB discussion postings.* Graham, B. (Ed.). Retrieved November 1, 2010 from http://www.metamute .org/en/Exhibiting-Locative-Media-CRUMB-discussion-postings

Cardiff, J. (2004–2005). *Her long black hair* [Artwork]. Retrieved November 1, 2010 from http://www.publicartfund.org/pafweb/projects/05/cardiff/cardiff-05.html

Chaos Computer Club. (2001). *Blinkenlights* [Artwork]. Retrieved November 1, 2010 from http://blinkenlights.net/

Davies, C. (1995). *Osmose* [Artwork]. Retrieved November 1, 2010 from www.immersence.com/

Davies, C. (1998). *Ephémère* [Artwork]. Retrieved November 1, 2010 from www.immersence.com/

de Souza e Silva, A., & Sutko, D. M. (in press). Theorizing locative media through philosophies of the virtual. *Communication Theory.*

Galloway, A. (2005). Urban mobile: At play in the wireless city [Presentation]. Pervasive and Locative Arts Network (PLAN) Event @ ICA, February 1–2, 2005, London, UK.

Galloway, K., & Rabinowitz, S. (1980). *Hole in space* [Artwork]. Retrieved November 1, 2010 from http://www.medienkunstnetz.de/works/hole-in-space/

Geser, H. (2004, March). Towards a sociological theory of the mobile phone. In *Sociology in Switzerland: Sociology of the mobile phone.* Zürich: Online Publications (Release 3.0). Retrieved November 1, 2010 from http://socio.ch/mobile/t_geser1.htm

Hewlett-Packard Development Company, LP (2007). HP's Mscape. Retrieved November 1, 2010 from http://www.hpl.hp.com/mediascapes

Hughes, N. (2009, August 27). Apple proposes location-based iPhone home screens. *AppleInsider.* Retrieved November 1, 2010 from http://www.apple insider.com/articles/09/08/27/apple_proposes_location_based_iphone_home _screens.html

Kellerman, A. (2006). *Personal mobilities.* London: Routledge.

Kirsner, S. (2005, May 23). One more way to find yourself. *The Boston Globe.* Retrieved November 1, 2010 from http://www.boston.com/business/technology/articles/2005/05/23/one_more_way_to_find_yourself/

Knowlton, J., Hight. J., & Spellman, N. (2002). *34 North 118 West* [Artwork]. Retrieved November 1, 2010 from http://34n118w.net/34N/

Laurel, B., & Strickland, R. (1992). *Placeholder* [Artwork]. Interval Research Corporation and the Banff Centre for the Performing Arts, United States. Retrieved November 1, 2010 from http://digitalarts.lcc.gatech.edu/unesco/vr/artists/vr_a_blaurel.html

Laurier, E. (2001). Why people say where they are during mobile phone calls. *Environment and Planning D, 19,* 485–504.

Longo, R. (Director). (1995). *Johnny Mnemonic* [Motion picture]. United States; Canada: TriStar Pictures.

Makimoto, T., & Manners, D. (1997). *Digital nomad*. New York: John Wiley & Sons, Inc.

NTT DOCOMO. (2003, March 27). *NTT DoCoMo to introduce first GPS handset* [Press release]. Retrieved November 1, 2010 from http://www.nttdocomo .com/presscenter/pressreleases/press/pressrelease.html?param[no]=215

Persson, P., Espinoza, F., & Cacciatore, E. (2001). GeoNotes: Social enhancement of physical space. In *CHI'2001: Conference on human factors in computing systems*, Extended Abstracts (Design Expo), Seattle, WA (pp. 43–45). New York: ACM. Retrieved November 1, 2010 from http://www.sics.se/ ~espinoza/documents/geonotes_chi_design_expo.pdf

Polak, E., & Auzina, L. (2004). *MILKproject* [Artwork]. Retrieved November 1, 2010 from www.milkproject.net/

Proboscis. (2002–2004). *Urban tapestries* [Artwork]. Retrieved November 1, 2010 from http://urbantapestries.net/

Rueb, T. (2001). *The choreography of everyday movement*. Retrieved November 1, 2010 from http://www.terirueb.net/choregraph/index.html

Rueb, T. (2005). *Itinerant* [Artwork]. Retrieved November 1, 2010 from http:// www.turbulence.org/Works/itinerant/index.htm

Rueb, T. (2007). On Itinerant. In Harrigan, P., & Wardrip-Fruin, N. (Eds.), *Second person: Role-playing and story in games and playable media* (pp. 273–277). Cambridge, MA: MIT Press.

Rusnak, J. (Director) (1999). *The thirteenth floor* [Motion picture]. United States: Columbia Pictures.

Siemens & Johannes Kepler University, Linz. (2005). *Digital graffiti*. Retrieved November 1, 2010 from http://w1.siemens.com/innovation/en/news _events/ct_pressemitteilungen/index/e_research_news/2008/index/e_22 _resnews_0823_2.htm

Spohrer, J. C. (1999). Information in places. *IBM Systems Journal, 38*(4), 602–628.

Tuters, M., & Varnelis, K. (2006). Beyond locative media: Giving shape to the Internet of things. *Leonardo, 39*(4), 357–363.

Waag Society (2002). *Amsterdam real time*. Retrieved November 1, 2010 from http://realtime.waag.org

Wellmann, B. (2001). Physical place and cyberplace: The rise of personalized networking. *International Journal of Urban and Regional Research, 25*(2), 227–252.

Wood, J. (2000). *GPS drawing*. Retrieved November 1, 2010 from www.gps drawing.com/

3

Social Networks and Games

Social interaction is enhanced by location awareness, and location aware-ness is enhanced by social interaction. Being aware of other people's presence and location in physical space is central to how we perceive spaces and to how we interact with others in those spaces. Before the existence of net localities, people could infer characteristics about certain spaces and people in spaces by talking to others who possessed firsthand experience or by reading about them in newspapers or magazines. But the increasing connectivity of localities enhanced by location-aware mobile technologies in public spaces has contributed to a new kind of social connection. In Chapter 2 we discussed how location-aware mobile devices are giving people the opportunity to access and contribute to the informational landscape that makes up net localities. In this chapter, we turn our attention to how a user's awareness of other people's locations in these spaces contributes to the formation of net localities. The ability to visualize not only the location of information and objects, but also of people nearby, transforms the way traditional social connections are developed, both in public and private spaces. It influences the spaces we might visit, and the people with whom we might connect. These types of location-aware applications are becoming increasingly popular, but, like most of the technologies we have discussed in this book, they have a long history of experimentation and development.

These technologies fall into two categories: location-based social net-works (LBSNs)[1] and location-based mobile games (LBMGs). LBSNs are similar to popular platforms like Facebook or Twitter,[2] only location is the central premise of interaction. Status updates include the location of the

Net Locality: Why Location Matters in a Networked World, First Edition. Eric Gordon and Adriana de Souza e Silva. © 2011 Eric Gordon and Adriana de Souza e Silva. Published 2011 by Blackwell Publishing Ltd.

user and social networks are organized by the physical proximity of users to one another. LBMGs are also social networks, but they have the added scaffolding of a game logic. For instance, a narrative that guides interaction, a task to perform, and some incentive system, such as points or badges. When people use mobile phones to connect to social networks through LBMGs, they are able to communicate and play with others in reference to their location. Most LBMGs lack a predefined game structure; that is, they do not have a clear end and are always running as long as there are users connected. Most importantly, gameplay often converges with "real" life. Anthropologist Johan Huizinga (1955) famously described the space of game play as the "magic circle," a space removed from the matters of everyday life. But the "magic circle" is not always clear – relationships and social encounters brazenly permeate both ordinary life and playful space. Instead of a digital space where players "meet" through digital avatars, a location-based gamer or social-network user can see the location of others on her mobile phone screen and choose to physically meet them if desired.

Both LBSNs and LBMGs are networked social environments, and as such they have origins in online multi-user environments. Created in 1978 by Roy Trubshaw and Richard Bartle, multi-user dungeons or domains (MUDs) were the first types of synchronous communication online environments. These systems allowed their users to talk to each other online, in real time. In this sense, they were social networks – but they were also games (Bartle, 1996). They included features such as tasks, rules, and goals that motivated people to play and participate in the community. MUDs became extremely popular in the early 1980s and spawned lots of similar systems from chat rooms to the more graphics-based MOOs (MUDs, Object Oriented).

As Torril Mortensen (2006) demonstrates, the early MUDs mutated into today's massively multiplayer online games, such as EverQuest and World of Warcraft. MUDs also inspired the development of online virtual worlds, like Active Worlds (1997) and Second Life (2003). As Dibbel (1999) explains, the link between these two types of online social spaces was TinyMUD, created by James Aspnes in 1989. An avid MUD player, Aspnes took the MUD game-like coding structure, but removed all the gaming elements, such as quests and killing – leaving only the opportunity for social interaction. From this perspective, online virtual worlds started as game worlds without the gaming structure. What was left was a (digital) space for social interaction.

Location-based games and social networks are descendants from these early online virtual worlds. The historical relationship between LBMGs and LBSNs is also similar to that between MUDs and TinyMUD. The first types of LBSNs were games such as Botfighters and Mogi – then LBMGs like Loopt and Brightkite emerged. They maintained the same structure of location-based games – interaction with others based on physical distance – but removed the gaming elements from the application. Interestingly, as we will see later, many of these applications have since added gaming elements to enhance participation.

Whatever the motivation to participate, it has become quite clear that the location of users is becoming influential on online social interactions. While games and online virtual worlds have been accused of isolating people from each other and from the "real" world, net localities are challenging that presumption. Digital networks are connecting us to the physical world and providing a framework for geographically located social interactions.

Scholars and artists have long emphasized the potential of location-aware mobile technology to create social environments and connect people in local spaces.[3] The realization that social exchange is central to how we understand our physical environment is profound, but not new. This chapter explores the artists, researchers, and companies that have contributed to the development of net localities by very early on realizing that the web, mobile phones, and games could connect people to one another in physical spaces and blur the boundaries between online and physical spaces.

Digital Connection in Physical Spaces

The first attempts at creating location-based social networks were the so-called "interpersonal aware devices." These devices used Bluetooth (short-length radio waves) to connect. So, instead of connecting a large number of users in many different locations, devices equipped with Bluetooth connect to other devices within short distances (1–100 feet). As a consequence, these early types of social networks were limited by proximity. The first interpersonal awareness device, called the Lovegety, was produced in Japan in 1998. The Lovegety was a wireless device small enough to be carried in someone's pocket or purse. If another Lovegety was detected nearby, the device would beep. If two interacting users had each turned on the dating feature, the device would make them aware of the gender and availability of the other. The Lovegety was an early attempt at bringing online dating and social networking into physical spaces.

Media artists built on this concept to create short-range interpersonal networks in physical spaces. Although many of the mobile-annotation pieces described in Chapter 2 allowed for the exchange of information among peers, they lacked the functionality of allowing participants to be aware of each other's presence in real time. Users could have access to the location of specific digital information and physical objects attached to locations by other users, but not to the users themselves. Works like Eric Paulos and Elizabeth Goodman's *The Familiar Stranger* (2002) and Katherine Moriwaki and Jonah Brucker-Cohen's *Umbrella.net* (2002) sought to change that.

Paulos and Goodman developed a Bluetooth-based mobile phone application called Jabberwocky that allowed users to visualize the location of nearby strangers. The application worked anonymously, that is, it didn't disclose personal information about users; rather, it sought to render public spaces more "familiar" by making users aware of strangers they had seen more than once. So, if a person carrying a mobile phone with the Jabberwocky software was in close proximity to another Jabberwocky user, the phone would record that. The next time these two people were in close range, the phone would alert both users. According to the artists' statement, the project's goal was to "improve community solidarity and sense of belonging in urban spaces."[4] Their intent was to show that strangers whom one consistently passes could be a familiar and comforting part of one's personal urban landscape.

Similarly, Moriwaki and Cohen's piece *Umbrella.net* explored the formation of ad-hoc networks and their potential for causing sudden and unexpected connections in urban spaces. The Dublin-based artists attached a Bluetooth-enabled handheld PocketPC (iPaq) to a series of regular umbrellas. When it rained, and the umbrellas were opened, the software created an ad-hoc network among the umbrellas, which allowed chat communication between umbrella users. According to the creators, "The umbrellas illuminate their states with bright LEDs. There are 3 states: 1) Pulsing red if searching for nodes, 2) Pulsing blue if connected to other umbrellas, and 3) Flashing blue if transmitting data between umbrellas."[5] Strangers in Paulos and Goodman's piece shared the Jaberwocky application, and strangers in Moriwaki and Cohen's piece shared the same type of Bluetooth-enabled umbrella. In each case, technology was employed to connect people who might otherwise not be aware of the other. Mobile devices were presented as social tools, and not merely as tools for managing one's personal information and networks.

Each of these pieces was influential in establishing the social possibilities of short-range connection in public spaces. Their contribution was simple: the desire for location included the desire to connect with others in location. A mobile device – the Lovegety, a mobile phone, or an umbrella – could be the interface for physical interaction. But these

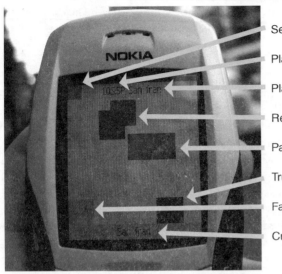

Searching On/Off

Places / Strangers

Place of Last Stranger

Recent Strangers

Past Strangers

True Stranger

Familiar Stranger

Current Place

Figure 3.1 Eric Paulos and Elizabeth Goodman's *The Familiar Stranger* (2002) mobile interface (Jabberwocky). Reproduced by permission of Eric Paulos and Elizabeth Goodman.

Figure 3.2 Jonah Brucker-Cohen and Katherine Moriwaki's *Umbrella.net* (2004). Reproduced by permission of Jonah Brucker-Cohen and Katherine Moriwaki.

systems were limited, as they could not connect the intricacies of one's immediate location to other remote locations.

Mobile social networks

A couple of years after the Lovegety was released, ImaHima was created in Japan. ImaHima, which means "Are you free now?" in Japanese, was an application for the i-mode standard mobile phone. Its creator Neeraj Jhanji claimed that he envisioned the application one day as he set out to have lunch by himself and wondered if any of his friends were nearby (Rheingold, 2002). He developed a service that allowed mobile phone users to broadcast their locations and receive text messages with updates of friends' locations. Around the same time, a similar service called Dodgeball was developed in the United States. Dodgeball, however, was not released commercially until 2005 when it was acquired by Google. Both Dodgeball and ImaHima had the common characteristic of allowing users to "broadcast" their current location to friends on their "buddy list" by sending an SMS to the application server. The server then distributed the message to the user's friends. However, none of these services relied on the mobile phone's location awareness or used mapping capabilities. So, although Lovegety, ImaHima, and Dodgeball aimed at connecting mobile users in physical spaces, none of them were "location-aware" per se.

ImaHima won the prestigious Net Vision/Net Excellence Prix Ars Electronica in 2001. While it enjoyed significant success within the somewhat rarified art world, it did not "cross over" into the mainstream. ImaHima and similar projects did a great job in facilitating the digital connection between people in physical spaces. However, they were not thoughtful in establishing a good reason to use them. There was no logic to user interaction. There was little motivation to participate in these systems outside of their novelty. It wasn't until game elements were added to the equation that the question of "why one would participate" began to be answered.

Games and Interaction

Games provide a logic for user interaction. While there are many ways of defining a game, LBMGs have consistent characteristics. Points or badges are awarded for different kinds of participation; competition and cooperation is designed into user interaction; or narrative is used to motivate play. Together, these kinds of features cultivate what Ian

Bogost (2007) calls a "procedural rhetoric," where participation is more about the procedure of participating than the content of any particular act of participation. For example, participating in a scavenger hunt motivates the player to move through the space of the hunt to find the next object on the list. The particularities of the space are not as important as the procedure of searching. Or consider the board game Monopoly. The game is about capitalism and real estate dealings, but rolling the die and collecting money structure game play. What motivates the player's interest is not the narrative, *per se*, but the rules of the game – the system of rewards and competition that surrounds the content.

The addition of game or game-like features into any system of interaction can potentially create user motivation to engage. This simple fact is quite important in the history of how interaction has been designed into location-aware devices. The first experiment with building a social platform using Global Positioning System (GPS) technology was a very simple game that was created almost by accident. On May 3, 2000, a computer consultant named Dave Ulmer wanted to test the accuracy of his new GPS device. He decided to hide a stash of videos, books, software, and a slingshot in the woods near Beaver Creek, Oregon, record its coordinates and post them online. He called it the "Great American GPS Stash Hunt," and sent a note to a GPS message board with one simple instruction: "Take some stuff. Leave some stuff." Within three days, two people found Ulmer's stash and documented their experiences online. By the end of the month, hundreds of people all over the world were hiding and finding things. And as the conversation grew, the name changed. The "Great GPS Stash Hunt" became known as Geocaching.

The premise of Geocaching has remained consistent since its inception, but the infrastructure around the practice has grown substantially. With nearly 800,000 hidden objects in over 100 countries, an entire subculture has built around what would seem a simple practice. Jeremy Irish, a Seattle-based web developer who started the site Geocaching.com, perpetuated much of this. Irish wanted to make it easier for the hobbyist to participate – so he created centralized discussion forums, a difficulty rating system, a database of caches searchable by name and location, and step-by-step instructions for how to get started. In addition, Irish began selling the necessary accoutrements to make sure caches were properly placed and protected, including waterproof boxes and logs. The most common objects found in these boxes are the two things sold on the site: geocoins and travel bugs. Geocoins are collectable objects that can be placed or removed from a cache and a travel bug is any object with a tracking tag. Many travel bugs have assigned tasks, such as to travel to 10 countries or

Figure 3.3 Geocaching Google Earth interface with different types of caches. © 2007 Google. © 2007 Europa Technologies.

find a body of water. The geocacher who finds the bug will carry it with them if they can help it complete its task. All movements of bugs and coins are recorded on the Geocaching site. Caches are classified according to how well they are hidden and the toughness of the terrain where they can be found. The traditional cache consists of a container and at least a logbook inside it. After finding the cache, the player signs the book and logs the find on the website.

The game logic is simple. You hide something and you find something. But in its simplicity, it makes an interesting point. It augments the physical world with hidden play pieces and provides a premise for which to travel through familiar and unfamiliar spaces. Players often plan entire vacations around finding caches – where locations, not tourist sites, become the motivation for travel. The game structures tourism and provides an overarching logic with which tourists can engage with the physical environment. But while Geocaching has clearly been effective in connecting people to locations, it has been less effective in connecting people to each other.[6] This began to change as mobile phones started to be used as interfaces for LBMGs.

In 2001, Swedish company It's Alive launched Botfighters, the world's first commercial LBMG.[7] Botfighters was open to the public, so anybody willing to pay for the mobile phone service could participate in the game, as long as they lived in the cities in which the game was running. The narrative of Botfighters followed the basic model of a first-person shooter (FPS) game, where the goal was to shoot and kill other players to acquire points and level up. The difference between Botfighters and a traditional FPS is that player interaction was based on physical location. Players could only interact in the game if they were sharing the same physical space.

After signing up for the game, players were notified via text message whenever another player was nearby. Players could respond by sending a reply with something like "shoot player x." The precision of their shot was dependent upon the type of gun they had and their physical distance to targets.

Botfighters ran for four years in countries such as Finland, Sweden, the United Kingdom, Ireland, and Russia. Some Botfighters players reported having experienced their city in unusual ways while playing the game. For example, Bjorn Idren, a Swedish Botfighters player, had this to say: "Eventually you start to take trips to places you wouldn't go to otherwise. I found myself sitting on the Web trying to find a nice café in an unknown part of Stockholm so that me and my girlfriend could have a picnic and also destroy a certain bot" (Mobile Killers, 2001).

Figure 3.4   Botfighters J2ME mobile and website interfaces by It's Alive! Reproduced by permission of Digiment Games Ltd.

The game was intended to influence patterns of mobility in the city, as well as to prompt players to forge new connections, both by having players imagine their everyday cities through the lens of a fictitious narrative, and also by motivating players to go to parts of the city to which they had never been. It sought to facilitate a simultaneously familiar and touristic approach to the city by establishing connections between local events and information and a larger network of activities taking place around them. It also sought to create a community of players both online and off. The procedural rhetoric of the game provided the motivation to move about the city; in addition, it provided the motivation for social interaction in locations that were independent of game play. The game rules got people to explore locations, but it was the resulting social encounters that enhanced location awareness.

Since Botfighters debuted, much more complex games have been built to enhance location awareness. The first project that combined mapping, real-time communication between local and remote participants, as well as the tracking of users' locations was a media art performance with game elements called *Can You See Me Now?* It was developed in 2001 by the

British art collective Blast Theory and the University of Nottingham's Mixed Reality Lab. It was a Pac-Man-style game in which players chased each other around the city. The real innovation of the piece was the splitting of the game space into two different environments: physical and digital, resulting in what some scholars have called hybrid reality games (de Souza e Silva, 2009). The first version of the game happened as a one-day performance in the city of Sheffield, United Kingdom. Because it was developed in 2001, *Can You See Me Now?* didn't use GPS phones. Instead it combined GPS devices for mapping location and walkie-talkies for communication. While Blast Theory players, equipped with GPS devices, PDAs, and walkie-talkies ran across the streets of Sheffield, online players from anywhere in the world logged onto a 2D web-based map of the city. From there, they were able to interact with the street players who were represented as dots on the map. Meanwhile, the street players could see the relative position of online players represented as white dots on a map of the same area on their PDA screens. The online players' goal was to run away from street players. But whenever a street player stood within five meters of an online player, they could be "captured" and forced to leave the game.

All the interactions amongst players were enhanced by some kind of communication. A live chat allowed online players to send text messages to other online players and to Blast Theory runners on the streets. And Blast Theory runners could communicate with each other and with online players via walkie-talkies. The communication was both strategic (Blast Theory members had a private backchannel for developing game strategies), and integral to crafting location awareness (they spoke about local weather conditions and the city's physical landscape to engage online players in the locality). Both types of players were occupying physical and online spaces, a kind of hybrid space created by the configurations of local and distant social connections.

Can You See Me Now? has become a seminal piece for all those studying the development of location-based games and location-based applications.[8] The game, which won the Golden Nica for Interactive Art at the Prix Ars Electronica Festival in Austria in 2003, has been performed around the world in cities such as Tokyo (2005), Rotterdam (2003), Chicago (2006), Barcelona (2004), and Oldenburg (2003).

In the newer versions of *Can You See Me Now?* the online game board is a 3D model of the city space and street runners are equipped with 3G GPS-enabled mobile phones. Blast Theory and the Mixed Reality Lab have continued their collaboration in the development of similar pieces, such as *Uncle Roy All Around You* (2003), *I Like Frank* (2004), *The Day of the Figurines* (2006), and *Rider Spoke* (2007). All of these projects sought to

Figure 3.5 Blast Theory's *Can You See Me Now?* (2001) mobile interface. Reproduced by permission of Blast Theory.

engage players with urban spaces, both locally and remotely, and to create new ways of accessing location-based information and interacting with strangers in urban spaces.

Games like Botfighters and *Can You See Me Now?* set the standard for subsequent projects such as Mogi in Japan. Mogi was a treasure hunt game in which players had to locate and collect virtual objects such as animals and fruit spread across the city of Tokyo. When a player was within 400 meters of one of these objects, they were notified. The goal of the game was to assemble a collection of like objects. Because Mogi was released in 2003, it accounted for what Justin Hall (2002) called a "second generation location-based mobile game": it ran on GPS-enabled mobile phones, which allowed an even more precise automated tracking of users' locations. Furthermore, like *Can You See Me Now?*, Mogi represented players on a 2D mobile map of Tokyo, so that users could actually "see" their physical distance to other players as a graphical representation on their mobile screen. This innovation was incorporated into Botfighters in Europe, Alien Revolt in Brazil (de Souza e Silva, 2008), and The Shroud in the United States later on. It is worth noting that small start-up companies developed all of these games. While they were indeed commercial and open to the general public, they were experimental in nature.

Christian Licoppe and Yoriko Inada (2006) studied the behavior of Mogi users in Japan. As with Botfighters, they found that players would frequently change their common patterns of movement through the city to play the game. For example, some players would take the bus instead of the subway on their daily commute to work in order to have a mobile phone

Figure 3.6 Mogi mobile and web interface. Reproduced by permission of NewtGames.

signal during the trip. Others would change their route to work to follow a path that included more virtual objects. Still others would make special trips during the evening hours to some part of the city they would not have otherwise gone, specifically to find virtual objects. Besides transforming how players interacted with locations, it also influenced how players perceived the co-presence of others. But this was not a good experience for all players. Some interpreted the persistent on-screen proximity of other players as a kind of stalking (Licoppe & Inada, 2009). When players felt that they could not be left alone, the comforting feeling of co-presence blurred with an anxious feeling of privacy lost. This study makes it clear that, in net localities, balancing the presence and absence of people and information is the hallmark of good design.

Inspired by games such as *Can You See Me Now?* and Mogi, PacManhattan (Lantz, 2004) was a game developed by Frank Lantz at the Interactive Telecommunications Program (ITP) at New York University (NYU). The premise of the game was the same as the popular 1980s arcade game,[9] only instead of using a joystick to manipulate a character on the screen, PacManhattan used real people for the characters and Manhattan for the playing board. Each game required 10 players, 5 running around the streets, assuming the personas of PacMan and 4 of his nemeses (Inky, Blinky, Pinky and Clyde), and 5 in a control room providing

Figure 3.7 Player running through Manhattan playing PacManhattan (April 2004) by Frank Lantz and the PacManhattan Team. Photograph © Dennis Crowley 2004. All rights reserved. Reproduced by permission of Frank Lantz and Dennis Crowley.

information to the players. The 5 characters on the street carried their mobile phones, each of which was being tracked via Wi-Fi hot spots. They then used the phones to be in constant contact with their counterparts in the control room, from whom they received updates on how many dots were still left on the board and where the other players were. While the technology would seem rather primitive by today's standards, PacManhattan provided some interesting insights into the relationship between urban spaces and game play. Many were surprised how players were perfectly capable of being fully immersed in game play even when major components of the game existed only virtually – on tiny screens or through voice communication. But this should not come as a surprise, since net locality has transformed immersion from a function of large screens and virtual reality to a function of small screens and the representation of located information and networks. Although this notion might seem contradictory or even absurd – in fact, we have always been immersed in physical spaces – the ability to overlay a fictitious narrative onto physical spaces and to forge local/remote connections in physical spaces contributes to a different perception of the spaces we inhabit. By looking at familiar spaces with the eyes of a tourist, and by finding new information and people in those spaces, people can become much more aware of the locations they inhabit.

Situated learning

In 2003 researchers at the Massachusetts Institute of Technology (MIT) began building augmented reality games (ARGs) to incorporate

the affordances of net localities into learning environments. ARGs transform mobile devices into a screen through which to view the physical
environment and augment reality with information. The group at MIT
sought to use the physical landscape to augment the kind of learning taking
place in the classroom.

There is a long history of games being used for learning across a range of
subjects.[10] Games have the unique capacity to engage participants in active
learning environments, where the learner becomes a participant and not
just a receiver of knowledge (Gee, 2007). In addition, they are considered
good learning activities because they engage students in social and experiential learning (Lave & Wenger, 1991; Kolb, 1984). Location-based
games offer an additional element: situated learning. By taking advantage
of the users' mobility and making use of location-aware interfaces, learning
activities can be situated in actual, relevant contexts (de Souza e Silva &
Delacruz, 2006; Klopfer, 2008).

As such, educational ARGs have been able to engage students in place-
specific simulations linked to a particular subject area. One of the first
educational ARGs, developed by Kurt Squire and Eric Klopfer, was
Environmental Detectives (ED) (Klopfer, Squire, & Jenkins, 2004). In
this, players sought to locate the source of a toxic chemical spill in a nearby
watershed. They used their mobile devices to check the spread of toxins,
take water samples, and interview fictitious characters to draw conclusions
about the chemical spill. Following Environmental Detectives, other
similar games were developed, such as Charles River City (MIT
Teacher Education Program, & The Education Arcade, 2004), and
Mystery at the Museum (MIT Teacher Education Program, & The
Education Arcade, 2003).

Simultaneous to the development of ARGs at MIT, educators at the
FutureLab in the United Kingdom created Savannah (FutureLab, 2003).[11]
It was a game in which middle-school students were supposed to learn about
animal life in the African savannah. Equipped with GPS-enabled devices,
students assumed the roles of savannah animals such as lions, elephants, and
zebras, and went out in the field. A simulation in their PDA told them
whether there were other animals (students) nearby, and if they needed to
defend themselves by connecting with other players. Remotely, the technical
team tracked the movements and communication of the students. So when a
student attacked another animal by pressing the "spray" button on their
PDA, the remote team could visualize the attack on their desktop computer.
They could then use this data to talk to the students about what happened
during the game. Savannah has several interesting implications for net
localities. As in *Can You See Me Now?*, players interacted with each other
during game play in such a way that was determined by their physical

Figure 3.8 Teachers in the Community Science Investigators' (CSI) workshop playing Environmental Detectives along the Charles River in Watertown, Massachusetts. Reproduced by permission of Eric Klopfer.

proximity. In addition, remote teams could track the progress and communication among students in the field. However, the game was place independent. That is, it could be played anywhere and so did not fully take advantage of the specificity of the environment.

Frequency 1550, developed by the Waag Society and educators at the University of Amsterdam (2005), took the idea of Savannah one step further. The goal of the game was to teach middle-school students about the history of Amsterdam. It was designed to get players exploring the physical spaces of the city, and to go places where historical events had happened. It was piloted during three days in February 2005.[12] Students (between 11 and 14 years old) were split into two categories: merchants and beggars. Each category was then divided into two teams: one team went on the streets of Amsterdam equipped with GPS-enabled 3G mobile phones and the other team stayed at a remote classroom location where they could help guide and interact with the students on the streets. Groups composed of online and street players set out to complete missions with the ultimate goal of gaining citizenship of the city of Amsterdam. So, for example, street players were required to find the location where an important battle took place, and take pictures from the place. In order to do that, they needed the help of the online players, who could access an

Figure 3.9 A group of children playing the game Savannah by Futurelab (2003) at the Bristol trial. Reproduced by permission of Futurelab.

online map of the city and guide street players to their destination. Groups accrued points by correctly completing each assignment. Whenever a group acquired 365 points, they would win the game.

Frequency 1550 used the physical spaces of the contemporary city to get players to engage with the past. The locations were instilled with the information required to make the past readable to the players. The information-rich locations were the context and content of learning. One of the goals of *Frequency 1550* was to situate the learning experience in the physical space. Because students interface with physical location and with each other through GPS-enabled mobile technologies, the idea is that learning occurs as a function of its context.

The Expansion of Location Awareness

With the release of the 3G iPhone and Droid in 2008, location awareness was propelled into the mainstream. Some of the initial applications that facilitated this were a mix of mobile annotation and LBSNs. For example, the Fwix application described in Chapter 2 also allowed users to add friends as "neighbors." This function allowed users to share stories with people in their network, creating a social element to annotation. The heat map on the phone indicated not only the frequency of popular press articles in a region, but also the location of status updates posted by neighbors.

Around the same time, other LBSN applications such as Loopt, Whrrl and Brightkite were developed. These applications inherited the location-based type of interaction from the experimental LBMGs described above, adding to that the standard social-networking logic: users post location-based updates and photos and are able to see friends' posts listed in order of proximity, as opposed to in reverse chronology which is typical of blogs and discussion forums. The result of these postings is a kind of narrative that develops around location.

For example, *Whrrl* users could post location-based updates and photos to a map interface. They could also see their friends' posts on a map. *Whrrl* users were encouraged to develop narratives around particular locations. ("What's your story?" was one of their taglines.) The idea was that users could share not just brief updates such as "I am here," but could combine numerous brief updates into a narrative that was connected to location. Writing a note about one's location is one thing ("beautiful sunset in Malibu this evening"), but something else happens when the located note is accessible to other people in that location. In sum, this dynamic relationship to location-based information is designed to influence how the user thinks about the space they are in while leaving a comment, how the user experiences location when augmented by their personal narrative or the narrative of others, and how the user might use others' narratives to form personal relationships. While the first influence is a characteristic of nearly all media (even print), the latter two are only found in location-aware applications (Sutko & de Souza e Silva, in press).

LBSNs combine awareness of other users' locations with the possibility of attaching information to places. Users are able to see each other's positions on their mobile phones and communicate with each other, similar to *Can You See Me Now?* and Mogi, but without the gaming component. Loopt (2008) was the first commercially available LBSN in the United States, though by the end of 2009, over 200 of them were in existence (Morgan, 2009). All of these applications had two common characteristics: first, they used the mobile phone's location awareness to automatically display a user's location, eliminating the need for self-reported position; and second, they had the ability to display, in real-time, users' locations on a map (de Souza e Silva & Frith, 2010). When a user opened Loopt, they were located with GPS tracking. They could look at a map and see if any of their friends were nearby. If friends logged in recently, their locations were marked on a map and the user could follow what they were doing via multimedia status updates. The status updates allowed people to post pictures of their location, letting friends "see" their physical surroundings.

Loopt also let people play an active role in locating friends by providing proximity alerts. For example, if a selected friend came within a certain physical distance, the phone set off an alert (Toldt, 2008). Like most LBSNs, Loopt allowed users to digitally annotate physical space. For example, if a member of the Loopt network was looking for a good restaurant downtown, she could log in and see if her friends left any reviews of the restaurants in her immediate area. She could then read those reviews and choose a restaurant based on the digital information attached to the physical space. LBSNs allow people to cooperate and use community-based knowledge to possibly change the perception of a space.

Many LBSN applications also encouraged users to meet "strangers" in public spaces, following the examples of the Lovegety and *The Familiar Stranger*. LooptMix allowed users to locate nearby users who were not previously known. Brightkite expanded this function and allowed a user to see the position of any Brightkite user within a block (200 m), in the

Figure 3.10 Citysense interface by Sense Networks for Blackberry. Reproduced by permission of Sense Networks, Inc.

neighborhood (2 km), in the area (4 km), in the city (10 km), or in the region (100 km). Taking the Brightkite idea a step further, the Citysense interface displayed groups of people represented as hotspots, but did not display individual users. Its interface displayed heat maps to illustrate spatial concentrations of users.

Although the first LBSNs were inspired by the early experiments with location-based gaming, they initially were not games. But by 2010 nearly all LBSNs added some element of gaming into their interaction strategy. Game elements have been incorporated into LBSNs to foster connections between users and to establish a context for connecting with locations. For example, Whrrl introduced "badges" and "societies" as tools for motivating participants. And Loopt launched what it called Loopt Star as a "mobile rewards game."

After Dodgeball was sold to Google in 2005 (and was subsequently shut down), its creators decided to develop another LBSN that incorporated a game logic. Foursquare commercially launched in the Spring of 2009. As of March 2010, the company reported over 725,000 users and 22 million check-ins.[13] That is significant growth, and is well beyond that of previous LBSNs. The reason is because it successfully combined the motivations of game play with the affordances of social networks. Foursquare offers

Figure 3.11 Foursquare interface for the iPhone. © Foursquare 2010.

points and badges for "checking in" to locations. Players are motivated to participate because these become public displays of one's accomplishments. The most powerful incentive is the chance of becoming mayor. The user who checks in most often to a location becomes the mayor of that location. This is valuable because each person who checks in subsequently is notified of the mayor's identity. If social networking operates in an economy of attention (Lanham, 2006), being mayor holds significant value. One's image and profile becomes a part of the information landscape of the location over which they preside. As silly as it seems, the opportunity to achieve symbolic political power motivates participation. Users are compelled to use Foursquare so that they can achieve this coveted position.

New Spaces, New Practices

Our spaces are no longer what they used to be. The development of mapping practices, the increased ability to attach information to places, and the growing interest in locating people and things in physical spaces are making net localities. Although we have always been aware of locations, the increasing popularity of mapping tools and location-aware mobile technologies are transforming the ways we experience locations, either remotely or proximately. And because spaces are inherently social (Lefebvre, 2001), reconfiguring spaces means reframing the social interactions within them.

Most of the artists, researchers, and early developers involved in creating the projects described in this chapter understood that location was a critical factor in shaping social interaction. But, these early experiments also challenged the traditional perception of face-to-face encounters as the only means of creating "true" interaction. Location matters, but our locations are now embedded within networked connections. And the social interactions motivated by those connections are part of our locations.

All the projects described in this chapter sought to bring the kinds of online community developed in virtual worlds to physical spaces. As a result, they began to make people aware that physical proximity was not the only characteristic of co-presence. Through these tools, people could be connected to others who were not physically present, and likewise, they could feel a greater sense of familiarity with them and their surrounding spaces. If people know something about the person next to them – even if it is only that they share the same route to work – they might be more inclined to develop some kind of connection with that person. Likewise, if people can access information about others who frequent certain places, they might also be able to infer qualities about specific localities and feel inclined to visit them.

Early LBSNs and LBMGs were certainly relevant to help establish and popularize today's location-based applications. But it is also true that once net localities become a reality for the majority of people in urban spaces (and not only for a select group of artists, researchers, and technology geeks), they will have significant implications for our understanding of urban spaces, privacy, surveillance, community, and globalization. We take up these matters in the remainder of the book.

Notes

1   This has also been described as locative mobile social networks (LMSN) by de Souza e Silva and Frith (2010).
2   Following the increasing popularity of location-based services (LBS), in 2010 both Facebook and Twitter added features that allow users to include their location in status updates.
3   See Hardey, 2007; Tuters & Varnelis, 2006; Hemment, 2004, 2006; Galloway & Ward, 2006; Vollrath, 2007a, 2007b; Levine, 2006; Shirvanne, 2007; Hight, 2006; Paulos & Goodman, 2003.
4   See Eric Paulos and Elizabeth Goodman's homepage at http://www.paulos .net/research/intel/familiarstranger/index.htm, retrieved on November 1, 2010.
5   See Katherine Moriwaki and Jonah Brucker-Cohen's project at http://www .undertheumbrella.net/system.htm, retrieved on November 1, 2010.
6   Although geocachers have formed very robust communities outside of the game. Most regions have regular meetups where "cachers" socialize face-to-face. There are also several online discussion forums devoted to the hobby. In addition, some types of caches were specifically designed to connect people, like the webcam cache. The webcam cache consists of the GPS coordinates of a public webcam. In order to document the finding, the player has to ask someone to monitor their computer screen while they stand in front of the webcam. The person monitoring the screen takes a screen shot of the player in front of the webcam and uploads it to the game's website.
7   See Sotamaa, 2002; de Souza e Silva, 2009.
8   See Flintham *et al.*, 2003; Benford *et al.*, 2006; de Souza e Silva & Hjorth, 2009; de Souza e Silva, 2009; de Souza e Silva & Sutko, 2008; Goggin, 2006.
9   PacManhattan wasn't the only classic arcade game adapted for located play. Tron, based on the arcade version of the movie, puts two or more players in a situation where they move through the city (tracked by a GPS device). Their urban path resulted in a digital trail, visible on the players' devices, which their opponents could not cross.

10 See de Souza e Silva, 2006; Delacruz, Chung, & Baker, 2009; Kahne, Middaugh, & Evans, 2008; Malaby, 2007; Kafai, 2006; Barab *et al.*, 2005.
11 See Facer *et al.*, 2004; Flintham *et al.*, 2003.
12 See Admiraal *et al.*, 2009; de Souza e Silva & Delacruz, 2006.
13 These statistics were taken from the official Foursquare blog at http://blog .foursquare.com/, retrieved November 1, 2010.

References

Admiraal, W., Akkerman, S., Huizinga, J., & van Zeijts, H. (2009). Location-based technology and game-based learning. In de Souza e Silva, A., & Sutko, D. M. (Eds.), *Digital cityscapes: Merging digital and urban playspaces* (pp. 302–320). New York: Peter Lang.

Barab, S., Thomas, M., Dodge, T., Carteaux, R., & Tuzun, H. (2005). Making learning fun: Quest Atlantis, a game without guns. *Educational Technology Research & Development, 53* (1), 86–107. Retrieved November 1, 2010 from http://inkido.indiana.edu/research/onlinemanu/papers/QA_ETRD.pdf.pdf

Bartle, R. (1996). Hearts, clubs, diamonds, spades: Players who suit MUDs. Retrieved November 1, 2010 from http://www.mud.co.uk/richard/hcds.htm

Benford, S., Crabtree, A., Flintham, M., Drozd, A., Anastasi, R., Paxton, M., Tandavanitj, N., Adams, M., & Row-Farr, J. (2006). Can you see me now? *ACM Transactions on Computer-Human Interaction, TOCHI, 13*(1). Retrieved November 1, 2010 from http://www.mrl.nott.ac.uk/~sdb/ research/downloadable%20papers/CYSMN%20tochi.pdf

Blast Theory, & The Mixed Reality Lab. (2001). *Can you see me now?* [Artwork]. Nottingham University, UK. Retrieved November 1, 2010 from http://www .canyouseemenow.co.uk/tate/en/intro.php#

Blast Theory, & The Mixed Reality Lab (2003). *Uncle Roy all around you* [Artwork]. Nottingham University, UK. Retrieved November 1, 2010 from http://www.blasttheory.co.uk/bt/work_uncleroy.html

Blast Theory, & The Mixed Reality Lab. (2004). *I like Frank* [Artwork]. Nottingham University, UK. Retrieved November 1, 2010 from www.ilikefrank.com

Blast Theory, & The Mixed Reality Lab, UK. (2006). *The day of the figurines* [Artwork]. Retrieved November 1, 2010 from http://www.blasttheory.co .uk/bt/work_day_of_figurines.html

Blast Theory, & The Mixed Reality Lab, UK. (2007). *Rider spoke* [Artwork]. Retrieved November 1, 2010 from http://www.blasttheory.co.uk/bt/work _rider_spoke.html

Bogost, I. (2007). *Persuasive games: The expressive power of videogames.* Cambridge, MA: MIT Press.

de Souza e Silva, A. (2006). Cyber to hybrid: Mobile technologies as interfaces of hybrid spaces. *Space and Culture, 9*(3), 261–278. DOI: 10.1177/ 1206331206289022 de Souza e Silva, A. (2008). Alien Revolt: A case-study of the first location-based mobile game in Brazil. *IEEE Technology and Society Magazine, 27*(1), 18–28. DOI: 10.1109/MTS.2008.918036

de Souza e Silva, A. (2009). Hybrid reality and location-based gaming: Redefining mobility and game spaces in urban environments. *Simulation & Gaming, 40*(3), 404–424. DOI: 10.1177/1046878108314643

de Souza e Silva, A., & Delacruz, G. C. (2006). Hybrid reality games reframed: Potential uses in educational contexts. *Games and Culture, 1*(3), 231–251. DOI: 10.1177/1555412006290443

de Souza e Silva, A., & Frith, J. (2010). Locative mobile social networks: Mapping communication and location in urban spaces. *Mobilities, 5*(4), 485–506.

de Souza e Silva, A., & Hjorth, L. (2009). Playful urban spaces: A historical approach to mobile games. *Simulation & Gaming, 40*(5), 602–625. DOI: 10.1177/1046878109333723

de Souza e Silva, A., & Sutko, D. (2008). Playing life and living play: How hybrid reality games reframe space, play, and the ordinary. *Critical Studies in Media Communication, 25*(5), 447–465. DOI: 10.1080/15295030802468081

Delacruz, G., Chung, G., & Baker, E. (2009). Finding a place: Developments of location-based mobile gaming in learning and assessment environments. In de Souza e Silva, A., & Sutko, D. (Eds.), *Digital cityscapes: Merging digital and urban playspaces.* New York: Peter Lang.

Dibbel, J. (1999). *My tiny life: Crime and passion in a virtual world.* New York: Henry Holt.

Facer, K., Joiner, R., Stanton, D., Reid, J., Hullz, R., & Kirk, D. (2004). Savannah: Mobile gaming and learning? *Journal of Computer Assisted Learning, 20*(6), 399–409. DOI: 10.1111/j.1365-2729.2004.00105.x

Flintham, M., Benford, S., Anastasi, R., Hemmings, T., Crabtree, A., Greenhalgh, C., Rodden T. A., Tandavanitj, N., Adams, M., & Row-Farr, J. (2003). Where on-line meets on-the-streets: Experiences with mobile mixed reality games. Proceedings of the SIGCHI Conference on Human Factors in Computing Systems, Fort Lauderdale, Florida, April 5–10, 2003, pp. 569–576.

FutureLab. (2003). Savannah [Game]. Retrieved November 1, 2010 from http://www.futurelab.org.uk/projects/savannah

Galloway, A. & Ward, M. (2006). Locative media as socializing and spatializing Practice. *Leonardo Electronic Almanac, 14*(3). Retrieved November 1, 2010 from http://leoalmanac.org/journal/vol_14/lea_v14_n03-04/gallowayward.html

Gee, J. P. (2007). *What video games have to teach us about learning and literacy.* New York: Palgrave.

Goggin, G. (2006). *Cell phone culture: Mobile technology in everyday life.* New York: Routledge.

Hall, J. (2002). Mogi: Second generation location-based gaming. *The Feature.* Retrieved November 1, 2010 from http://thefeaturearchives.com/100501.html

Hardey, M. (2007). The city in the age of Web 2.0: A new synergistic relationship between place and people. *Information, Communication and Society, 10*(6), 867–884. DOI: 10.1080/13691180701751072

Hemment, D. (2004). The Locative Dystopia. In *Freedom of Movement,* Makeworlds Paper No. 4. Retrieved November 1, 2010 from http://www.makeworlds.org/node/76

Hemment, D. (2006). Locative arts. *Leonardo, 39*(4), 348–355.

Hight, J. (2006). Views from above: Locative narrative and the landscape. *Leonardo Electronic Almanac, 14*(7/8), 9.

Huizinga, J. (1955). *Homo Ludens.* Boston, MA: Beacon Press.

Kafai, Y. B. (2006). Playing and making games for learning: Instructionist and constructionist perspectives for game studies. *Games and Culture, 1*(1), 34–40.

Kahne, J., Middaugh, E., & Evans, C. (2008). *The civic potential of video games* [White paper]. The MacArthur Foundation. Retrieved November 1, 2010 from http://www.civicsurvey.org/CERG_Publications.html

Klopfer, E. (2008). *Augmented learning: Research and design of mobile educational games.* Cambridge, MA: MIT Press.

Klopfer, E., Squire, K., & Jenkins, H. (2004). Environmental detectives: PDAs as a window into a virtual simulated world. In Kerres, M., Kalz, M., Stratmann, J., & de Witt, C. (Eds.), *Didaktik der Notebook-Universität.* Münster: Waxmann Verlag.

Kolb, D. A. (1984). *Experiential learning: Experience as the source of learning and development.* Englewood Cliffs, NJ: Prentice Hall.

Lantz, F. (2004). PacManhattan [Game]. Retrieved November 1, 2010 from http://pacmanhattan.com/

Lanham, R. (2006). *The economics of attention: Style and substance in the age of information.* Chicago, IL: University of Chicago Press.

Lave, J., & Wenger, E. (1991). *Situated learning: Legitimate peripheral participation.* Cambridge: Cambridge University Press.

Lefebvre, H. (2001). *The production of space.* Oxford: Blackwell.

Levine, P. (2006). Art and GPS. *Leonardo Electronic Almanac, 14*(3/4), 3.

Licoppe, C., & Inada, Y. (2006). Emergent uses of a multiplayer location-aware mobile game: The interactional consequences of mediated encounters. *Mobility, 1*(1), 39–61.

Licoppe, C., & Inada, Y. (2009). Mediated co-proximity and its dangers in a location-aware community: A case of stalking. In de Souza e Silva, A., & Sutko, D. M. (Eds.), *Digital cityscapes: Merging digital and urban playspaces* (pp. 100–128). New York: Peter Lang.

Malaby, T. M. (2007). Beyond play: A new approach to games. *Games and Culture, 2*(2), 95–113.

MIT Teacher Education Program, & The Education Arcade. (2003). Mystery at the museum [Game]. Retrieved November 1, 2010 from http://education.mit.edu/ar/matm.html

MIT Teacher Education Program, & The Education Arcade. (2004). Charles River City [Game] Retrieved November 1, 2010 from http://education.mit.edu/drupal/ar/projects#crc

MIT Teacher Education Program, & The Education Arcade. (2004). Environmental detectives [Game]. Retrieved November 1, 2010 from http://education.mit.edu/ar/ed.html

Mobile Killers. (2001, 15 July) *Sunday Herald Sun.* 1st edn., p. 89.

Moriwaki, K., & Brucker-Cohen, J. (2002). *Umbrella.net* [Artwork]. Retrieved November 1, 2010 from http://www.undertheumbrella.net/system.htm

Morgan, T. (2009). How consumers are really using location. Proceedings of Where 2.0 Conference, May 19–21, 2009, San Jose, California.

Mortensen, T. E. (2006). WoW is the new MUD: Social gaming from text to video. *Games and Culture, 1*(4), 397–413. DOI: 10.1177/1555412006292622

Paulos, E., & Goodman, E. (2002). *The familiar stranger* [Artwork]. Retrieved November 1, 2010 from http://www.paulos.net/research/intel/familiar stranger/index.htm

Paulos, E., & Goodman, E. (2003). *The familiar stranger: Anxiety, comfort, and play in public spaces.* Berkeley, CA: Intel Research.

Rheingold, H. (2002). *Smart mobs: The next social revolution.* Cambridge, MA: Perseus.

Shirvanne, L. (2007). Social viscosities: Mapping social performance in public space. *Digital Creativity, 18*(3), 151–160.

Sotamaa, O. (2002). All the world's a Botfighter stage: Notes on location-based multi-user gaming. In Mäyrä, F. (Ed.), *Proceedings of Computer Games and Digital Cultures Conference.* Tampere: Tampere University Press.

Sutko, D. M., & de Souza e Silva, A. (in press). Location-aware mobile media and urban sociability. *New Media & Society.*

Toldt, A. (2008). Verizon and Loopt team up. *eFluxMedia.* New York.

Tuters, M., & Varnelis, K. (2006). Beyond locative media: Giving shape to the Internet of things. *Leonardo, 39*(4), 357–363.

Vollrath, C.J. (2007a), Seeing what's important: Mapping strategies in locative media. Paper presented at the Annual Meeting of the NCA 93rd Annual Convention TBA, Chicago, Illinois.

Vollrath, C.J. (2007b) The uncanny impulse of locative media. Paper presented at the International Communication Association (ICA) Annual Meeting ICA, San Francisco, California.

Waag Society. (2005). *Frequency 1550* [Artwork]. Retrieved November 1, 2010 from http://freq1550.waag.org/

4

Urban Spaces

Cities are comprised of net localities – they are teeming with people and data. And as these spaces continue to grow in influence, we need to consider how they are changing the nature of being in the city. Many critics have lamented the decline of public spaces as they have become cluttered with outside connections, drawing positive correlations between global connections and local disconnections (Goldberger, 2007). Environmental psychologist David Uzzell (2008) has declared that technology use in public space is equivalent to a virtual crime against humanity, where "places are being stolen right from under our noses." The cultural critic Howard Rheingold (2002, p. xxii) observed that on trains and buses in Japan passengers preferred to talk to somebody who was physically absent than with other people who were in the same vehicle. With the popularization of mobile phones, this claim has become common sense. Mobile phones promote social disruption, especially when used in public spaces such as restaurants and public transportation.[1] Critical theorist Norman Klein has suggested that when people talk on a mobile phone while walking, they move through physical space, but they are actually not there.[2] Psychologist Kenneth Gergen (2002) called this "absent presence." It is when "one is physically absorbed by a technologically mediated world of elsewhere" (p. 227). And according to Klein, this "generates a culture of tremendous paranoia and isolation. The more we promote an invasion of privacy in public spaces, the more we make ourselves isolated from the world around us."

Still, people continue to occupy urban spaces and continue to use them in imaginative ways. When spaces are both physical and digital, and when

Net Locality: Why Location Matters in a Networked World, First Edition. Eric Gordon and Adriana de Souza e Silva. © 2011 Eric Gordon and Adriana de Souza e Silva. Published 2011 by Blackwell Publishing Ltd.

interactions between people are mediated, this does not spell the end of good urban spaces; but it does spell a change. Decisions about what to pay attention to are being made in very different ways; the purview of what is near has expanded beyond that which is right next to you, and paying attention to an anonymous user at a neighboring street corner, visualized on a mobile map, is just as likely as paying attention to the stranger across the street. This phenomenon does present a challenge to commonly held attitudes about urban space. As so forcefully argued by urban historians and activists over the last several decades, good urban spaces are a product of co-located individuals engaging in any variety of social rituals and interactions, resulting in stronger communities and safer streets.[3] When mediated interaction is added to the equation, the apparent cohesion of urban space is, indeed, brought into question. If someone is talking on a phone, sending a text message, checking their mobile map, or uploading a Wikipedia article, they may forget to smile at a passer-by or properly thank the street vendor from whom they purchased a pretzel. While the use of mobile devices in public might reduce the frequency of these familiar, polite, social rituals, it is simultaneously extending and modifying those rituals into less familiar contexts.

Contemporary society has created new contexts for interaction, not all of which are solely determined by being in the same physical space. Mediated by location-aware technologies, co-presence can extend beyond the physical into a networked environment. People can be aware of others' presence through markers on a map or a local tweet.[4] "It is progressively more common to navigate two spaces simultaneously," argue Kazys Varnelis and Anne Friedberg (2008), "to see digital devices and telephones as extensions of our mobile selves." The web is brought into the spaces we occupy, and, similarly, those spaces are brought into the web. But this takes practice. The ability to navigate two spaces simultaneously is actually the ability to consolidate and locate the spaces and information that we associate with our "digital selves" into something of a hybrid space. Hybrid spaces are "social situations in which the borders between remote and contiguous contexts no longer can be clearly defined" (de Souza e Silva, 2006). The mere existence of location-aware devices in cities does not create net localities; net localities are practiced spaces – they develop over time, through social practices with technology. What's more, they include all those people who are co-present in the physical space who are not accessing digital information. The woman walking down the street without a device, not accessing information, becomes part of the situation that comprises the space. These spaces can be quite flexible.

Even so, some critics take a hard stance against any digital connectivity in public. Some have argued that any networked connection in an urban space removes the user from that space, removes them from the context of public, and places them squarely within their familiar networks, thus posing a serious threat to the urban space and the social capital that would be built and exchanged there (Wellman, 2002; Hampton, Livio, & Goulet, 2010). This anxiety about technology mediating distance is nothing new. According to Lilli Zeuner, sociologist Georg Simmel, in describing technologies like the telescope and the microscope at the start of the twentieth century, suggests that they transform what was "instinctive or unconscious" into something "more sure but fragmented. ... What was distant before now comes closer, at a cost of greater distance to what was previously closer" (Zeuner, 2003, p. 81; see also Simmel & Frisby, 2004). And many critics have applied this idea to the mobile phone. It has been argued that mobile phones build confidence and connection to that which is distant, but they do so at the expense of that which is near.[5]

This position too firmly establishes a normalized urban space that technology is disrupting. However, urban spaces are always mediated by technology. Buildings, cars, streets, signs – these are all technologies that contribute to the experience of a city street. Net localities, while surely an augmentation of the traditional urban space, are comprised of additional technologies that help to form urban spaces. They produce unique inter-actions and, by extension, new contexts for social cohesion. Co-presence is not mutually opposed to networked interaction – and as emerging practices of technology develop, drawing that line in the sand becomes increasingly difficult.

Good Ol' Public Spaces

Questions about urban public space have been vigorously debated for at least a century. Simmel (1971) noted that the rapid increase in external stimuli found everywhere in the city was constructive of a new urban subject, one capable of blocking things out at will and developing what he called a "blasé attitude." This metropolitan man, as he described it, was rational and calculating. To accommodate everyday life (talking to strang-ers, buying food, or commuting to work) he had to exercise a kind of mental reserve. The city was incomprehensible in its unfiltered form, so having mental reserve was required to separate out the various social situations from the sites and sounds of the urban street. The "blasé attitude" was a coping device that people adopted to deal with the realities of urban life. While Simmel was highly critical of this new urban subjectivity, he acknowledged the unprecedented freedom enjoyed by the metropolitan man. Life in the metropolis forced a seemingly unnatural rationalization of everyday life, but at the same time it enabled a freedom to become something different and break the bonds of small town life.

Fast forward 100 years, and Simmel's observations still resonate. At the time of Simmel's writing, he noted that the city, and its associated technologies, forced individuals to mentally adapt to its form. Urban subjectivity was a new way of approaching the world. Anonymity and increased sensory stimulation became a regular part of everyday life. And he recognized that there was no turning back. He made it clear that the metropolitan man can never return to the small town, as he would feel too restricted. The smaller the social circle, "the more anxiously the circle guards the achievements, the conduct of life, and the outlook of the individual." In the metropolis, the individual reigned supreme. The personal freedoms enjoyed in the metropolis were seductive – even if it required a complex assortment of new technologies to realize them.

There is no doubt that the blasé attitude still exists – we place limits on what we take in through our senses. We consciously choose to avoid looking at a homeless man or the electronic billboards that surround us, and we employ new technologies to assist in that filtering. Maps and mobile devices are useful interfaces through which to engage the seemingly incomprehensible world around us. As more of the world's information is available online, it is possible for us to outsource some of that filtering to our mobile devices.

This produces net localities. As we employ technologies to assist in filtering, we produce more information to be filtered. We even reorient the nature of the space. Urban space extends into the web and vice versa. As Eric Gordon argues in *The Urban Spectator* (2010), new technologies always prompt a change in urban subjectivity and urban form, and not necessarily to the exclusion of what came before. Urban spaces are constantly changing to accommodate new tools and practices. The introduction of photography altered how people looked at cities, and so, too, did the popularization of film. The rapid increase and accessibility of web data marks another important shift in urban spaces. Net localities have proliferated because of technologies that enable urban practices to extend beyond what one can touch or see. Of course, there are consequences to each technological shift and there is a period of social realignment where social norms adjust to the realities of everyday life.

Sociologist Barry Wellman has pointed to a change in social interactions that he calls "networked individualism" where people connect directly to one another through the network, but not to the physical space surrounding them. Others have noticed trends of "telecocooning" (Habuchi, 2005) or "selective sociality" (Matsuda, 2005), where small groups of friends interact via mobile digital networks and ignore the larger public sphere. The web has introduced new platforms for interaction and those platforms are almost certainly altering interactions in public spaces. But just as we can characterize this trend as a propagation of the worst elements of online life, where human connections are rationalized into computer code and public isolation, we can also understand this as yet another shift in the meaning of urban space and the freedoms (perceived or otherwise) associated with that space. Traditional metropolitan public space is perhaps becoming like the small town, where pure physically co-present social circles seem oppressively small. Not being connected to a network, not having access to information about where you are, is tantamount to being closed off to a space's potential. Along the lines of Simmel's metropolis, net localities encourage a new social organization that produces self-protectionism; but at the same time, it produces a sense of freedom. The person participating in a net locality is not limited to what immediately surrounds her; she has the ability to associate with a much wider swath of information and people. Even Simmel recognized that the metropolis expanded the who and what of social interaction. While we are still dependent on social groups, he says, "It has become a matter of choice with whom one affiliates and upon whom one is dependent" (p. 130). Before net locality, the city made it possible to self-select people and spaces with which to associate. The rise of net localities makes this kind of selectivity the prominent characteristic of city space.

But as net localities become the norm, they are not necessarily normalized; they still might appear disruptive or strange in the larger social context. From the outside, they might appear to be dead spaces, collections of co-located individuals with nothing to say to one another. But, in fact, there is a great deal of nuance in these spaces – a great deal of social exchange that is slowly carving out the rules and conditions of this new space. To understand them, we need to look at specific practices of socialization taking place within them. How are people using technologies to engage with the proximate and the remote simultaneously? What rules of conduct are assumed in these engagements and what new rules are emerging that expand the possibilities of urban spaces?

Traditionally, urban spaces have been viewed as self-contained places. Good interactions with public spaces have been considered those which were also limited to physical contiguity. As the architectural critic Paul Goldberger asserts, "You are not on Madison Avenue if you are holding a little object to your ear that pulls you toward a person in Omaha" (2007). Good public space, in this respect, is a space to which one gives their undivided attention.

Paying absolute attention to any one thing requires one to trust that there is no risk in not paying attention to other things: at risk of personal harm, or risk of missing something important. But there are different kinds of trust: trust in a close friend or a spouse and a more generalizable trust in "the way things work." Robert Putnam (2000) calls the latter "thin trust." Distinct from *thick trust*, or "trust embedded in personal relations that are strong, frequent and nested in wider networks," *thin trust* involves "the generalized other" and "rests implicitly on some background of shared social networks and expectations of reciprocity" (Putnam, 2000, p. 134). So, while thick trust is what makes you trust your spouse when they say they are going to pick up the kids, thin trust is what makes you trust that the person walking down the street is not going to stab you. Likewise, trust in an urban space, the kind that leads to undivided attention (or the intention of achieving it), might include trusting in familiar people that occupy the space (neighbors, friends, shopkeeper), but it also likely includes thin trust in the anonymous people who occupy the street, perhaps even the street itself.

Thin trust can be divided into two categories: thin trust in institutions or technologies and thin trust in the users of those institutions or technologies. In the first category, as it pertains to net localities, there needs to be trust in all the technologies involved in the situation – that means, the streets, buildings, and signage, as well as any digital interface that may be used to interact with the space. We have a generalized trust in operating systems, applications, and particular functions within applications. We trust our work lives and, increasingly, our social lives to the continual functioning of these technologies. The second category of thin trust is the generalized trust in the people using the technologies. Trusting that someone talking on a mobile phone is acceptably present in a situation, and not mentally disturbed, requires not only a trust in the technology, but also a trust in how that person is using it. We have a generalized trust that the phone will not be used to ignite a bomb just as we have a generalized trust that automobiles on the road will not cross over into opposing traffic or drive onto the sidewalk. While these things *do* happen, while there are breaches in this trust, they are rare enough so that we can still generally trust users to behave in ways that are conducive to functional urban space.

Effectively, public space is a collection of minor social contracts, where the experience of the whole is determined by the relative intactness of the constitutive parts. But, indeed, the complexity added to any public space by virtue of mobile devices is going to pose challenges to the established rituals developed for physical interaction. And it requires that the participants in any public space share a general understanding of the technologies being brought to bear on the situation. If someone were to bring a hologram machine into a subway, for instance, the situation would almost certainly be disrupted by the novelty of the technology. There would be no baseline from which to build trust. As mobile devices are becoming a regular part of our social landscape, they can now be accepted into the general framework of social interactions, making it possible for specific technologies to alter the situation, without disrupting it. The sociologist Randall Collins (2004) argues that co-present situations are dependent upon participants being "mutually aware of each other's focus of attention" (p. 48). By that he means that their focus of attention must be co-located in a physical space. But as location-aware technologies are further normalized, mutual aware-ness of attention will take place in a variety of ways, from the verbal "uh huh" as someone is talking, to the meandering dot on a Loopt map. But, how people communicate to one another that they are sharing a space, and how they integrate the information from technologies into the social rituals that compose space depends on the situation.

Here's the situation

We turn to sociologist Erving Goffman (1963) to clarify the actual practice of these minor social contracts that define net localities. This might seem like a counter intuitive approach, as Goffman was a theorist of face-to-face interactions, concerned primarily with a unit of analysis he calls the "situation," or "the full spatial environment anywhere." But while Goff-man pays little attention to mediated interactions, he provides a very productive framework from which to approach the problem. There are social rituals that compose every situation; these rituals are organized by a set of expectations and the performances born of the meeting of those expectations.

Goffman admits that the society has an expectation that urban spaces be comprised of each individual's undivided attention. But he is quick to point out that engagement, even in important matters like urban space, is highly variable, and typically consists of two kinds of involvement: dominating and subordinate. "A dominating involvement," according to Goffman, "is one whose claims upon an individual the social occasion obliges him to be ready to recognize; a subordinate involvement is one he is allowed to sustain only to the degree, and during the time, that his attention is patently not required by the involvement that dominates him" (1963, p. 44). In urban spaces, the situation manufactured by the physical composition of things and people is dominating in most cases. When we are standing right next to others, even in non-intimate contexts like a public street, we expect the dominating involvement to be the physical space and the nearby person. However, in net localities, we acknowledge that there are other outlets for involvement, and we accept them, insofar as they don't interfere with the established order of the dominating involvement.

When a person sending a text message while walking bumps into somebody else, this is an obvious affront to social expectations. When a person moves to the side of a crowded sidewalk to send that text message, the correspondence between the dominating and subordinate involvements is not as clear. That person is ostensibly removing themselves from their dominating involvement with the physical space, but they have not caused any harm or inflicted any injury. They are, however, seemingly ignoring their obligation to participate in the outward appearances of a space that feels truly public. We do this all the time, with or without the aid of mobile devices. Reading on a train removes a person from the dominating involvement of the space. Walking around with an iPod functions the same way. Even daydreaming on a street corner can momentarily "take someone away." But there is a middle ground created when a person "goes away," but does so while maintaining the dominating involvement of the local space. Goffman recognizes that when people look as *though* they are coming from someplace or going to someplace, they exhibit an "objective that leaves the actual focus of attention free for other things; one's destination, and therefore one's dominant involvement, lie outside the situation" (1963, p. 56). In this case, there is a disconnect between the typically dominant involvement of the physical space and the person's focus of attention which rests outside of it. But what happens when the person's attention is focused on the map of where they happen to be standing, or a person in their social network that happens to be down the street? The dominating involvement is not limited to the physical situation – it is clear that the physical situation remains integral to the larger situation. Looking at nearby restaurant reviews on an iPhone map momentarily distract one's attention, but with the goal of applying that distraction to the physical situation. While it might appear that the person is "lolling," as Goffman calls it, they are, in fact, deliberately extending the purview of the local situation.

But perhaps it does not matter. Looking down at a device in a situation where other co-present individuals expect that you exhibit attention to the physical space might appear disruptive, regardless of individual intent. The user, then, is often responsible for maintaining two separate situations, each with a set of rules that need to be followed. In physical space, there is a rule against "'having no purpose,' or being disengaged." As a result, users appropriate "untaxing involvements to rationalize or mask desired lolling – a way of covering one's physical presence in a situation with a veneer of acceptable visible activity" (1963, p. 58). This might mean sitting on a bench, or stopping in a nearby alcove with one's mobile phone. In the context of net localities, there are rules as well. There is etiquette for stopping what you are doing and checking in to a location-based social network, and there are prohibitions against ignoring someone in your network that is "very close." If someone is one block away, it is rather rude to ignore that person. This situation would require that the user cover up their involvement by appearing "otherwise engaged." Perhaps an update such as "I'm in a meeting," or, "Rushing to get the train." In net localities, the local space is the dominating involvement; however, the local space is not always solely physical. In the physical space of the street, the technology is brought to bear on one's assessment of the "situation." Local space is the dominating involvement, even as one's attention is directed to a screen.

Within net localities, therefore, the coherence of the physical situation remains, while the user's attention is freed up to an ecology of foci that are not only tolerated, but constructive of the experience and appearance of urban space. That person on the street might be sending a text message to a colleague halfway across the world, but they also might be searching for information about where they are standing, in the form of restaurant reviews or urban history, or communicating with a person who happens to be in the coffee shop across the street. The composition of net localities can tolerate a wide variety of attentional foci as long as the physical situation is not disregarded (as in the case of the texter running into somebody else). In fact, as the accepted norms of urban space shift to accommodate this variety, expectations will shift along with them. Net localities are spaces where one *can* shift their attention outside of the physical situation, because the situation is understood to be larger than what is physically near.

"Getting Away with Going Away"

While Simmel lamented that the metropolis forced individuals, as a condition of their freedom, to shield themselves with a blasé attitude – a way of (dis)engaging with the world characterized by a rational and calculating reserve, Goffman approached the problem of continued and intense involvement in urban public spaces from a different, yet complimentary angle. Instead of assuming permanent changes in a mental state to deal with the consistently chaotic state of the metropolis, Goffman noticed that, in public social situations, people grasp on to opportunities to momentarily escape. He called this "going away."

> When outwardly participating in a social activity within a social situation, an individual can allow his attention to turn from what he and everyone else considers the real or serious world, and give himself up for a time to a playlike world in which he alone participates. This kind of inward emigration from the gathering may be called "away." (1963)

Away, for Goffman, meant a mental retreat into another space. It meant not being in the situation. It didn't, however, necessarily imply a disruption to the situation. Individuals can "get away" while the social ritual that organizes the situation remains in tact. For instance, letting one's mind wander on a crowded sidewalk is often aided by looking at a billboard, a magazine, or a mobile phone. Goffman called this "getting away with going away" (1963, p. 70). We focus attention on things in the physical environment to create the impression that we are only momentarily distracted from the situation.

Or, increasingly, it is not uncommon for people to begin from the state of "away" so that they have control over when they return. Take, for example, the use of earbuds and an MP3 player on a crowded street corner. If one runs into a casual acquaintance while waiting to cross a street, and that acquaintance has white buds dangling from his ears, he has permission to behave somewhat differently in the situation. He can smile and nod, while keeping the earbuds in place, and then turn his head away once again. Or, if he really wanted to talk to the interlocutor, he could remove his earbuds and engage in the kind of small talk that would normally be required for this casual connection. If, on the other hand, he didn't have the earbuds at all, and didn't want to be insulting, he would have to go with the latter option. Social conventions would restrict him from turning away and ignoring the encounter all together. In this case, the technology provides a means of filtering the city, or creating an outward appearance of the reserve to which Simmel referred, but in such a way that empowers the individual to engage in the situation on his own terms.

In this example, the individual starts from the position of away, and instead of getting away with going away, he is getting away with *being* away. And his dominating involvement is likely someplace other than the local situation. This example demonstrates how wielding control over the terms of engagement is important for an individual's sense of mastery over a space, but may not be conducive for good public spaces. Net localities, on the other hand, are spaces in which individuals wield control of information, while keeping their dominating involvement local. Even as they "go away" from the physical situation to review messages on their iPhone, they are using the local to organize their involvement in the digital interface. While there are still social regulations that organize the physical and digital spaces independently of one other, because the dominant involvement is the same, there is a relaxation on the level of policing that each situation receives. If three people are walking down a street looking for a restaurant and one of them "goes away" to look at the Yelp iPhone application that finds nearby restaurant reviews, it is easy for him to "get away with going away," as his leaving the physical situation is understood as being in service to the net locality.

As Goffman explains:

> In public, we are allowed to become fairly deeply involved in talk with others we are with, providing this does not lead us to block traffic or intrude on the sound preserve of others; presumably our capacity to share talk with one another implies we are able to share it with others who see us talking. So, too, we can conduct a conversation aloud over an unboothed street phone while either turning our back to the flow of pedestrian traffic or watching it in an abstracted way, with the words being thought improper; for even though our co-participation is not visually present, a natural one can be taken to exist, and an accounting is available as to where, cognitively speaking, we have gone, and, moreover, that this "where" is a familiar place to which we could be duly recalled should events warrant. (1981, p. 86)

Goffman is talking about mediated conversations. But what's important in this example is not what's on the other end of that unboothed street phone, but that the person talking on the phone has gone away somewhere familiar. As long as the other people in the situation understand where he has gone, the act of going away is less likely to disrupt the situation. In a net locality, if one goes away as a means of enhancing local interaction and convincingly demonstrates the continuity in their dominating involvement, then it is quite easy to "get away with going away."

Consider this example: a woman is sitting in a café sharing a cup of coffee with her friend. Just as she begins to respond to a question about her family, her phone, which is sitting on the table, buzzes; the woman pauses her sentence midstream and looks down at her phone to see the incoming message. She tilts the phone at a 30-degree angle to view the screen, sees that she has been pinged by a person who happens to be at a restaurant across the street and who saw her update on Foursquare. She pauses for a brief moment, sends off a quick text message, and puts the phone down. Her friend, noticeably disturbed, settles back in her chair while her friend sends the message. As soon as she is finished, she explains that her other friend, a mutual acquaintance, is nearby and wants to stop by to say hello. After this explanation, the tension is quickly broken and the conversation turns to how this mutual acquaintance is doing. In this example, the situation was significantly altered by this "interruption," but because the excuse for going away was directed at the local situation, it was quite easy for her to get away with it.

Now consider this: that same woman is sitting in that same café talking to that same friend. In mid sentence, her phone rings. She stops, looks at the incoming number, and answers the call. She lifts a single finger and silently mouths "one moment" to her physically co-present friend. She proceeds to talk on the phone about plans for the upcoming weekend to her friend on the phone. In this case, she turns her dominating involvement away from the local space with little intention of covering up her absence. She keeps the conversation short and returns to the physical situation with "I'm sorry about that, I've been trying to connect with her for weeks." Her friend smiles and they continue talking. While the phone call did not permanently disrupt the situation, and the woman showed deference to her physically co-present friend, she did not integrate the phone call into the local situation. There are a number of ways this encounter could have played out, from relatively innocuous to downright rude (Plant, 2001), but in the example above, the phone call was disconnected from the local situation. The phone call is taking place in spite of the space. In net localities, despite one's need to "go away" to engage with a device, going away reinforces the dominant involvement with the local.

There are many ways to use technology to either limit or expand a social situation. Keith Hampton and Neeti Gupta (2008) study the use of public Wi-Fi in coffee shops as a means of discovering some of them. Their study produced mixed results. On one hand, they warn against what they call "public privatism." It is possible, they argue, that "public Wi-Fi will consist of private cocoons of interaction that benefit existing close ties, distract from interactions with co-present others, and ultimately reinforce the existing trend toward privatism." But they also contend that the opposite may be true – that people might use the technology to engage more deeply in the places they occupy. In their study of cafés in Boston and Seattle, they identified two types of Wi-Fi users: true mobiles, for whom the coffee shops functioned as a "backdrop for activities focused on the completion of work," and placemakers, who "used their laptops as a premise to enter and engage in the 'social hubbub' of the space." Whereas true mobiles use their laptops as a shield against public interaction, placemakers use their laptops as an excuse to integrate into the scene. They seem eager to engage in conversation about what they're doing and provide openings, like looking up from their screens and even turning their screens so that others can see. The true mobile goes away in the device in spite of the local situation, whereas the placemaker goes away to attract local attention. This study is instructive, in that it calls attention to varied approaches to the same technology – in this case, the laptop. The difference between approaches lies entirely in the intention of the user and how those intentions are communicated within the context of the local situation. In other words, it is all about performance.

Performance In/Of Public

Information is not just something to consume. One's awareness of nearby information (and people) can also be a context for performance. When urbanist William Whyte described "good public space," he referred to the Seagram Building plaza in Manhattan, where "on a good day, there would be a hundred and fifty people sitting, sunbathing, picnicking, and schmoozing – idly gossiping, talking 'nothing talk'" (1980). For Whyte, the publicness of the space was the outward appearance of people engaging with one another, even if those engagements had no content ("nothing talk"). Architects and urban designers have so completely bought into this representation of public that, for decades, they have tried vigorously to reproduce similar spaces, if not in actual fact than only in appearance, by designing pedestrian intersections and street furniture to produce the appropriate impressions (Leccese, McCormick, & Congress for the New Urbanism, 2000). This conceptualization of public has a long history in the digital realm as well. Since the 1990s, designers of chat rooms, MUDs (multi-user dungeons or domains), and MOOs (MUDs, Object Oriented) have represented spaces that gave the impression of being public (Dibbell, 1993; Rheingold, 1993). In LambdaMOO, for example, private spaces were referred to as "bedrooms," and public spaces as "living rooms." The intention was to create spaces for idle talk, for serendipity, where in the spirit of "good public spaces," people would just happen upon one another.

So, while good public spaces were spaces that invited idle chatter, great public spaces were spaces that mandated it. Whyte refers to the plazas in Rockefeller Center in midtown Manhattan as a great space. It is great because it maintains its publicity through performance. Despite popular opinion, he says,

> The lower plaza is only one part, and it is not where most of the people are. They are in the tiers of an amphitheater. The people in the lower plaza provide the show. In winter, there is skating; in summer, an open-air café and frequent concerts. The great bulk of the people – usually about 80 percent – are up above: at the railings along the street, along the mezzanine level just below, or on the broad walkway heading down from Fifth Avenue. (Whyte, 1980, p. 59)

While praising the space, he laments that it is often misunderstood. Architects are constantly borrowing from the design of the plaza, but as means of creating a space for crowds, they typically reproduce only the lower plaza, without its context. "They wind up having a stage without a theater, a hole without the doughnut. And they wonder what went wrong" (1980). Watching a performance (or performing), whether official or unofficial, is part of what makes public spaces work. Watching the ice-skaters from Fifth Avenue is an acceptable form of going away. And, indeed, ice-skating at Rockefeller Center, as a kind of performance, is

Figure 4.1 The upper and lower plazas at the Rockefeller Center at Christmas time. Photograph © Ed Yourdon 2009, http://creativecommons.org.

also a kind of going away. In the ideal situation, the occupant of the space can move near seamlessly between these two practices.

Goffman (1959) acknowledges the importance of performance in everyday interactions. He goes so far as to use the analogies of a stage with its front and back regions. When on stage, people behave in a manner dictated by the rules and regulations of a performance. Actors remain loyal to the script and the audience expects that they do so. But they do not have to always remain on stage; they may retreat backstage where social regulations are not quite as policed. After a scene, an actor may leave the stage and complain to the stagehands that the "audience seems really dead tonight." And yet, when he returns onstage, he is expected to conceal this opinion. In one example, Goffman describes a waiter. The waiter behaves differently when in the dining room (front region) than when in the kitchen (back region). He speaks to the patrons of the restaurant in one way and he speaks to the other waiters and kitchen staff in quite another. What is interesting about this situation is that all the actors understand the distinction between the front region and back region. The restaurant patrons know that the waiter might retreat backstage and speak in a different manner; and of course the kitchen staff know that the waiter will have to perform when he goes "onstage." The performance remains stable just as long as the regions do not blur. If the kitchen conversation were to be overheard in the dining room, the performance would be disrupted. So consider again what makes Rockefeller Center work. It's not just that there are the two plazas: one for the performer and one for the audience. But it is a "great public space" because one doesn't have to remain on or off stage. There is fluidity between the two spaces – where performance can become voyeurism, and voyeurism can become just an appearance of voyeurism as one attends to other matters. And each act of performance and voyeurism references the other. The local situation is central.

The sociologist Joshua Meyrowitz (1985) provides an interesting addendum to Goffman's formulation. He contends that Goffman too heavily relies on physical metaphors for his explanations and, in fact, the distinction between the front and back regions can also be prescribed by "information flows." The movement between front and backstage in Goffman's example is quite literally tied to space. The actor has to move from one space to another. But Meyrowitz contends that "the patterns of information-flow, whether direct or mediated, help to define the situation and the notions of appropriate style and action" (1985). In other words, the nature of the performance, while partly determined by the physical setting of the plaza, can be influenced by an informational change in the situation. For example,

Meyrowitz uses the example of the waiter's boss walking into the kitchen. All of a sudden, the backstage transforms into the front; the relaxed social regulations corresponding with the kitchen conversation are now transformed, and the waiter is forced to reconfigure his performance accordingly. Or in some cases, we might imagine that instead of the binary between front and back, there is reason to construct what Goffman calls a "double-front stage" (Goffman, 1959).

But instead of two stages, per se, net localities require performing for two audiences on one stage. Playing a game like Botfighters (described in Chapter 3), for example, necessitates that the player performs for other players while she simultaneously performs for bystanders sharing the physical street. That Botfighters players could be at the other side of the city, or sharing the same street block, complicates the situation. So, the distinction between local and remote is blurred, since even remote players can be digitally co-present on the player's mobile phone screen and therefore "participating" in the local situation. Additionally, there is another tension that arises between physically co-present people, who might or might not be part of the game. The distinction between players and bystanders is complicated. Even though bystanders are likely not playing the game, they are integrated into the space by virtue of being part of a game audience. However, in some cases, this audience is pulled into the game space. For example, in the game *Uncle Roy All Around You* (Blast Theory, & The Mixed Reality Lab, 2003), street players are supposed to ask for information from people on the streets in order to find the location of Uncle Roy's office. Likewise, players of Botfighters might get directions from strangers in order to find a place where a "robot" (another player) is. If an anonymous stranger is influencing the outcome of the game, is that person considered part of the game or the game audience?

Foursquare (discussed in Chapter 3) is an instructive example. It is built on small performances. When a user "checks in" to a location, they are announcing their presence in a space. Metaphorically, this is like inhabiting the lower plaza while one's "friends" gather around to observe. While physically occupying a given space, the person checking in needs to perform to the mediated audience and as such needs to go away for the amount of time it requires to check in. Though one could argue that this practice primarily serves to disengage the performer from the situation, it is possible to say the same about the ice-skater at Rockefeller Center. The dominating interest of the ice-skater is clear and observable; and the dominating interest of the Foursquare user is less clear. However, the outcomes are comparable. Whether standing on Fifth Avenue or using Foursquare, the space of the performance becomes the spectacle for the observers and the space of the observers becomes the context from which the public space garners meaning. While the design of physical space matters for the organization of social situations, these examples demonstrate that information flows can be equally as influential. With this, Whyte's concern about the architect's lack of consideration for the variable spaces of performance is brought into relief. Just as people often misunderstand the functionality of the plazas at Rockefeller Center, so too do people misunderstand how information flows influence the possibilities for engaging in a space. There is evidence that people are becoming more brazen with their use of technologies in urban spaces, choosing remote contacts over proximate connections (Gournay, 2002; Habuchi, 2005). But there is also evidence that going away does not require turning one's back on the local situation. When this happens, it is a net locality and not simply a locality disrupted by a network. As the use of location-aware technologies continues to expand in urban spaces, the nature of spaces, and, in time, the nature of the city will change.

Transformed Urban Spaces

Simmel (1971) ends his 1901 essay "The Metropolis and Mental Life" with this: "Since such forces of life have grown into the roots and into the crown of the whole of the historical life in which we, in our fleeting existence, as a cell, belong only as a part, *it is not our task either to accuse or to pardon, but only to understand*" (emphasis added). Likewise, we seek to understand net localities so that we might begin to understand how to use them to design and inhabit great public spaces. People are using technologies in a variety of ways and on a regular basis, bringing the reality of network access to bear on everyday interactions in urban space. In some cases, they are using these tools to distance themselves from public space, "getting away with being away," but in other cases, they are using the tools to expand the purview of public space by bringing local information in networks to bear on local physical space. What we want to communicate here is that the pervasiveness of location-aware technologies in public spaces does not necessarily lead to their disintegration. Net localities provide a counter example for all of those who decry the effects of technology on public space. Public urban spaces are far too complex to diagnose. There are many uses for urban spaces and location-aware technologies are opening up more of them. Good, vibrant public spaces have to accommodate these tools and become a platform for the various modalities of engaging with local life – including community participation and civic engagement. And, if the rules of access to net localities are in the hands of the people who design these platforms for social interaction, how can policy makers and the public influence these design decisions that will literally shape our public spaces? The next chapter explores some possible answers to this question.

Notes

1 See Ling, 2004; Gergen, 2002; Hampton, Livio, & Goulet, 2010.
2 Interview with de Souza e Silva (Nov. 8, 2002).
3 For social rituals and interactions see Whyte, 1980; Jacobs, 1969; for stronger communities see Leccese, McCormick, & Congress for the New Urbanism, 2000; Haas, 2008; Putnam, 2000; for safer streets see Jacobs, 2002.
4 Licoppe and Inada (2006) call this an onscreen encounter. What's interesting about these encounters is that they don't exist in opposition or even in parallel to physical co-presence, but increasingly, they are experienced in dialogue with the physical situation.
5 See Gergen, 2002; Puro, 2002; Plant, 2001; Habuchi, 2005.

References

Blast Theory, & The Mixed Reality Lab. (2003). *Uncle Roy all around you* [Artwork]. Nottingham University, UK. Retrieved November 1, 2010 from http://www.uncleroyallaroundyou.co.uk

Collins, R. (2004). *Interaction ritual chains.* Princeton, NJ: Princeton University Press.

de Souza e Silva, A. (2006). From cyber to hybrid: Mobile technologies as interfaces of hybrid spaces. *Space and Culture, 9*(3), 261–278.

Dibbell, J. (1993, December 23). A rape in cyberspace: How an evil clown, a Haitian trickster spirit, two wizards, and a cast of dozens turned a database into a society. *The Village Voice,* New York. Retrieved November 1, 2010 from http://www.villagevoice.com/2005-10-18/specials/a-rape-in-cyberspace/1/

Gergen, K. (2002). The challenge of absent presence. In Katz, J., & Aakhus, M., (Eds.), *Perpetual contact: Mobile communication, private talk, public performance* (pp. 227–241). Cambridge: Cambridge University Press.

Goffman, E. (1959). *The presentation of self in everyday life.* New York: Anchor.

Goffman, E. (1963). *Behavior in public places: Notes on the social organization of gatherings.* New York: Free Press.

Goffman, E (1981). *Forms of talk.* Philadelphia: University of Pennsylvania Press.

Goldberger, P. (2007, February 22). Disconnected urbanism: The mobile phone has changed our sense of place more than faxes, computers and e-mail.

Metropolis Magazine. Retrieved November 1, 2010 from http://www .metropolismag.com/cda/story.php?artid=254

Gordon, E. (2010). *The urban spectator: American concept-cities from Kodak to Google.* Hanover, NH: Dartmouth College Press.

Gournay, C. de (2002). Pretense of intimacy in France. In Katz, J. E., & Aakhus, M., (Eds.) *Perpetual Contact* (pp. 193–205). Cambridge: University of Cambridge Press.

Haas, T. (2008). *New urbanism and beyond: designing cities for the future.* New York: Rizzoli.

Habuchi, I. (2005). Accelerating reflexivity. In Ito, M., Okabe, D., & Matsuda, M., (Eds.), *Personal, portable, pedestrian: Mobile phones in Japanese life* (pp. 163–182). Cambridge, MA: MIT Press.

Hampton, K., & Gupta, N. (2008). Community and social interaction in the wireless city: Wi-fi use in public and semi-public spaces. *New Media and Society,* *10*(8), 831.

Hampton, K. N., Livio, O., & Goulet, S. (2010). The social life of wireless urban spaces: Internet use, social networks, and the public realm. *Journal of Communication, 4,* 701–722.

Jacobs, J. (1969). *The death and life of great American cities.* New York: Modern Library.

Jacobs, J. (2002). *The death and life of great American cities.* New York: Random House.

Leccese, M., McCormick, K., & Congress for the New Urbanism. (2000). *Charter of the new urbanism.* New York: McGraw Hill.

Licoppe, C., and Inada, Y. (2006). Emergent uses of a multiplayer location-aware mobile game: The interactional consequences of mediated encounters. *Mobilities, 1,* 39–61.

Ling, R. (2004). *The mobile connection: The cell phone's impact on society.* San Francisco, CA: Morgan Kaufmann.

Matsuda, M. (2005). Mobile communication and selective sociality. In Ito, M., Okabe, D., & Matsuda, M., (Eds.), *Personal, portable, pedestrian: Mobile phones in Japanese life* (pp. 123–142). Cambridge, MA: MIT Press.

Meyrowitz, J. (1985). *No sense of place: the impact of electronic media on social behavior.* New York: Oxford University Press.

Plant, S. (2001). *On the mobile: The effects of mobile telephones on social and individual life.* Motorola. Excerpt retrieved November 1, 2010 from http://www.cyborganthropology.com/On_the_Mobile

Puro, J. P. (2002). Finland: A mobile culture. In Katz, J., & Aakhus, M., (Eds.), *Perpetual contact: Mobile communication, private talk, public performance* (pp. 19–29). Cambridge: Cambridge University Press.

Putnam, R. D. (2000). *Bowling alone: The collapse and revival of American community.* New York: Simon & Schuster.

Rheingold, H. (1993). *The virtual community: Homesteading on the electronic frontier.* Reading, MA: Addison-Wesley.

Rheingold, H. (2002). *Smart mobs: The next social revolution.* Cambridge, MA: Perseus.

Simmel, G. (1971). *"The metropolis and mental life," on individuality and social forms; selected writings.* Ed. D. N. Levine. Chicago, IL: University of Chicago Press.

Simmel, G., & Frisby, D. (2004). *The philosophy of money.* 3rd edn. London and New York: Routledge.

Uzzell, D. (2008). People-environment relations in a digital world, *Journal of Architecture and Planning Research, 25*(2), 94–105.

Varnelis, K., & Friedberg, A. (2008). Place: The networking of public space. In Varnelis, K., (Ed.). *Networked Publics* (pp. 15–42). Cambridge, MA: MIT Press.

Wellman, B. (2002). Little boxes, glocalization, and networked individualism. In Tanabe, M., van den Besselaar, P., Ishida, T. (Eds.). *Digital cities, LNCS 2362* (pp. 10–25). Berlin and Heidelberg: Springer-Verlag.

Whyte, W. H. (1980). *The social life of small urban spaces.* New York: Project for Public Places Inc.

Zeuner, L. (2003). *Cultural sociology from concern to distance.* Trans. S. Harris. Copenhagen: Copenhagen Business School Press.

5

Community

In his book *Bowling Alone*, the sociologist Robert Putnam (2000) argues that Americans are disengaging from one another. As the metaphor in the title implies, they continue to participate in things, but they are not doing it together. They are bowling, but not in leagues. He argues that civic engagement is quickly diminishing from the everyday life of Americans, and people are not participating in the traditional structures of society with the frequency they once did. They are less likely to vote, participate in neighborhood meetings, or volunteer for a local organization. In the year 2000 when the book came out, all indicators were grim, and according to Putnam, civic engagement is at risk. It is threatened by, among other things, suburbia and television and every other technology that might separate people from one another.

In 2010, Putnam, with his colleague Thomas Sander, published a follow up article to the book entitled "Still Bowling Alone?" where they note a reversal in this trend. The "post 9/11" generation of young people, they argue, is reengaging. The 2004 and 2008 presidential elections in the United States marked a resurgence in youth participation in the political process. Youth were more frequently discussing politics with one another and they expressed a greater optimism about their ability to effect change in the country. Sander and Putnam associate this shift with the national trauma of 9/11 and suggest that it evoked a positive awareness of the role of government and nation among young people and brought them together around a common wound.[1]

Of course, it is quite difficult to associate causality with this shift in youth attitudes. As they note in their article, the rise of social networking software

Net Locality: Why Location Matters in a Networked World, First Edition. Eric Gordon and Adriana de Souza e Silva. © 2011 Eric Gordon and Adriana de Souza e Silva. Published 2011 by Blackwell Publishing Ltd.

has surely had some effect. And, blogging, mobile connectivity, and other social technologies cannot be overlooked. While some have continued to disparage the rapid growth of digital communication as a noxious influence on social life, disrupting more traditional forms of communication, other commentators are quite optimistic about how these media have forged close associations among youth and motivated them to participate in political and social life.[2] Sander and Putnam (2010) are cautiously optimistic about digital media, noting that "such technological civic invention is in its infancy," and that real work is needed for online tools to produce "real and enduring civic effects" (p. 15) – especially if they are to address the social gaps that they have no doubt helped to create.

To understand the correlation between networked technologies and political participation, we have to look at the implications of location awareness. Sander and Putnam do not take into consideration the blurring between the web and locations. They continue to see the web as this other space that might craft pro-social behaviors, as opposed to a tool that people have incorporated into their lives to accomplish the tasks of everyday life. If we are to really take a close look at why people, especially youth, are more engaged in public life, we cannot ignore the affordances of net localities on civic action. As people become location aware, they can also become aware of the political impact of locations. We have addressed this already with changes in public urban spaces. Now, we want to address this in terms of civic engagement. How does net locality motivate civic action? How does it invest people in their neighborhoods and their communities? And, importantly, what are the threats associated with it in terms of ossifying existing gaps in participation?

Community and Society

Location awareness is factoring into community life in a myriad of ways – in everything from mass protests to neighbors communicating with each other online to people engaging with government services. We point to a trend in local life in cities where people and governments are employing the affordances of net localities to organize and (hopefully) improve their communities. But, of course, this is not without controversy. Some contend that this kind of communication is having adverse effects on local communities. As we described in Chapter 4, this argument is based on a rich history of scholarship that associates technology with local community disruptions. In the 1920s, Robert Park (Park, McKenzie, & Burgess, 1925) argued that while new communication technologies, like the telephone, expanded opportunities for social interaction, they had a corrosive effect on local social ties. People were speaking more, but not to the people right next to them. This is a familiar critique that seems to be resurrected with each new technology that enters into neighborhood life. Televisions were blamed for isolating people, as they converted the living room into a private public sphere (Spigel, 1992; Meyrowitz, 1985), and the web was blamed for making it far too easy for people to connect with those outside of their locality (Kapor, 1993). More recently, mobile phones (as we discussed in previous chapters) have been accused of harming public places by prioritizing the distant over the proximate (Katz & Aahkus, 2002; Moores, 2004; Plant, 2001).

We do not want to wholly discount these critiques. But, too often, this anti-technology sentiment relies on a faulty premise of technologically aided communication replacing an ideal form of community that existed before it. The nineteenth century German sociologist Ferdinand Tönnies (2002) referred to this ideal form as *Gemeinschaft*. Gemeinschaft (loosely translated as "community") is a collective social form premised on folk culture and strong ties. It suggests a way of life that is natural, spontaneous, and harmonious, which he associated with the way human relations ideally should be – intimate, enduring, static, and moral. Gemeinschaft is a naturally occurring community whose members are bound together by concentrated bonds of kinship, fellowship, shared history, beliefs, and commonality. In Tönnies' view, the Gemeinschaft community with its strong mechanisms of social support was the source of solidarity within small towns and pre-industrial society. In contrast, *Gesellschaft* (in its most pejorative sense) is society. It is "opposed to [Gemeinschaft] in veiled hatred and contempt" (p. 252). Gesellschaft is characterized by differentiation, dissimilar ways of life, and rational interactions that occur largely through self-interest and formal contracts. In short, Gesellschaft is the city. People are bound together via spatial organization rather than by tradition and shared history; behavior is regulated by the enactment of formal laws rather than social norms. Tönnies believed that Gesellschaft has completely dominated social life, and there are only fleeting remnants of Gemeinschaft still observable.

But this narrative of "community lost" is too simple. It is deeply problematic to assume that all technological additives to community life destroy the underlying cohesion of community. The telephone, the telegraph, the automobile, the elevator, and the mobile phone have all played some part in reorganizing social life – connecting people through physical and virtual space *and* providing justification for disconnection. They have, each to a certain extent, increased social connectivity *and* social isolation at the same time.

The web is no different. Only, more than other technologies, it is built on the rhetoric of community. In fact, the word community is so overused that is hardly tolerable anymore. In the popular media, most web activities are referred to as online communities, from a small email listserv to the entirety of Facebook. So, community is not the same thing as Gemeinschaft. Gemeinschaft is an ideal, while community is popularly understood as any online network of people. The reason the web is so often associated with the demise of Gemeinschaft is that the two meanings of the term are too often aligned. If Facebook in general is the new community, then we do have something to fear. Community has become meaningless. But, if certain uses of social networking sites like Facebook can aid groups of neighbors, family, and friends to correspond in ways that enhance their sense of solidarity, then this is something entirely different. This, we argue, is what can take place in net localities.

But, of course, it would be equally wrong-headed to assume that net localities are the new form of Gemeinschaft. Net localities do represent a rationalization of local life. They translate local information and knowledge into machine-readable data. They organize the custom-based orientation of localism into an algorithmic system that can be used and amplified. But, by virtue of motivating geographically local communication, they also mobilize the ubiquitous form of online community with the more rarified impulses of Gemeinschaft. They combine the affordances of constant connectivity with the daily, ritualized routines of a locality.

So how are communities organizing themselves to accommodate the needs of their local spaces? How are governments assimilating or resisting the affordances of net localities? There has been rapid growth in the use of locally oriented online social spaces, such as online forums, virtual worlds, and location-aware applications for phones. These online spaces are factoring into everyday life in neighborhoods and reorganizing the traditional relationships of neighbor to neighbor. Additionally, news is increasingly being produced by local community members rather than by established news outlets. And local governments are creating means of civic participation by incorporating social networking and transparency in data access into their list of essential services. These new platforms for social interaction reconfigure the way people engage with each other in their local communities.

Neighborhood Connectivity

When we think about what it means to live in an active and engaged neighborhood, we often think about parks, local coffee shops, front porches, and community centers. A web forum does not typically come to mind. However, in a growing number of neighborhoods around the world, online interaction is important for neighborhood engagement. While the networks created with these technologies have traditionally been the exclusive territory of affluent neighborhood associations – historically, email listservs have been used to extend existing neighborhood associations (Kahlenberg, 2005) – this is changing. By 2009, web saturation in North America reached 74.1% – a 134% rate of growth since 2000 (Internet World Stats). This suggests a significant increase in the diversity of people connected. While affluent neighborhoods are still more likely to use the web for neighborhood business, the gap is shrinking. More people have high speed internet in their homes and it is increasingly easy to adopt social tools such as Google Groups, Yahoo! Groups, and email listservs.

The digital scaffolding offered by these tools changes the dynamics of local participation. First of all, they resist the top-down localism linked to the traditional neighborhood association. Instead of going through a central organization, people in online forums can communicate in unstructured or less structured networks. It allows casual conversation to merge with official conversation (Hampton & Wellman, 2003; Hampton, 2007). And, there are very low transaction costs associated with connecting with neighbors. One does not need to pay dues, or potentially confront someone face-to-face. But the content of the exchanges is not ultimately what is important; rather, the mere presence of communication on these forums creates an awareness of an existing community that can lead to a more sustained connection to a local network of people.

While the online forum for communication increases the ease and frequency of conversation, the local, place-bound connection assures a certain care in transactions. In a local context, people communicating online typically use their real identity, and they either already know each other or have the potential of meeting each other on the street (and are therefore likely to have information about other users' personality or manner).[3] As such, misunderstandings and "flame wars" are less likely in these situations (Kavanaugh *et al.*, 2005), enabling the forum to function in a supporting, not leading role, in community formation.

Several empirical studies support the notion that neighborhood forums actually serve to increase the communication activity within neighborhoods.[4] Online forums can provide a kind of scaffolding or support to routine local interactions: a public reminder of a sidewalk conversation or a report of a crime. Posting typically does not replace face-to-face correspondence; it amplifies it. It does this, not by deepening connections, but by extending them to more people. Sociologists make a distinction between strong ties and weak ties. Strong ties include family and close friends, and weak ties are typically professional associates, people who share interest, and neighbors. Keith Hampton points out that, in fact, "Not only are strong, intimate ties with neighbors the exception, but the presence of many weak ties may be extremely beneficial and an over-abundance of strong ties may be limiting" (2007, p. 719).[5] Neighbor-hoods are not where are all your friends live. Nor is that desirable. Too many strong ties in a locality can lead to provincialism and the kind of oppressive small town culture that sociologist Georg Simmel (1971) warned against, where apparently local concerns blanket the global or systemic issues facing a locality.

Adding some networked component to neighborhood life is not a panacea for urban ills. But, good communication among neighbors has a strong correlation to other indicators of neighborhood cohesiveness (Jeffres, 2008). While there is considerable variability among neighbor-hood cohesiveness based on socioeconomic conditions, levels of mobility, poverty, segregation, and home ownership, good communication is an element that can mitigate some of these disadvantages. Some have argued that these disadvantages make the implementation of neighborhood for-ums far less effective (Kavanaugh *et al.*, 2005). But others have demon-strated that because the transaction costs of communication are so low within a digital forum (for instance, there is no social commitment as with face-to-face or telephonic communication), contextual factors such as poverty and segregation have little effect on the frequency and efficacy of digital communication within a neighborhood context (Hampton, 2010).

Consider the case of i-Neighbors, which started as a research project out of the Annenberg School for Communication at the University of Penn-sylvania. Launched in 2004 in the United States and Canada, i-Neighbors spread only through word of mouth and currently houses over 30,000 users comprising over 6,000 "digital neighborhoods" from a wide diversity of socioeconomic neighborhood profiles. In a recent study of the plat-form, 50 of the most active neighborhoods in the system were analyzed (Hampton, 2010). Out of those 50 neighborhoods, the majority were middle-class suburbs, but 28% were classified (based on 2000 census figures) as having concentrated disadvantage, defined as extent of racial segregation (measured as the percentage who were black), percentage of residents below the poverty level, and unemployment rate. While it has been previously demonstrated that digital neighborhood forums within middle-class suburban neighborhoods lead to increased levels of social cohesion and collective action (Hampton & Wellman, 2003), the i-Neighbors study shows that, in fact, even in neighborhoods of concentrated disadvantage, the levels of social cohesion and informal social control exhibited in the use of the digital system are equal to that exhibited in more advantaged neighborhoods (Hampton, 2010).

As these forums become more prominent in neighborhood life, and as they cross over socioeconomic boundaries, there is an even greater social need for their distribution to be equitable. Power is exercised, as Manuel Castells (2009) points out, "not by exclusion from the networks, but by the imposition of the rules of inclusion" (p. 43). In other words, net localities can result in a desire for strengthened local cohesiveness just as they can redefine what it means to be cohesive. This is a problem. The rules of net localities are imposed equally upon those communities with and without the means to adopt the appropriate technology. Even if a community is not equipped to engage in digital communication, they will be expected to do so. This is an interesting by-product of the web. The more extensive its reach, the more power it wields in its impression of totality (Gordon, 2010). As more and more localities find their place in the network, there is increased pressure to play by the rules of the established system.

This puts the digital divide argument into a different perspective. It is not simply a matter of technological infrastructure bypassing a certain portion of the population. The infrastructure for these tools is fairly well established, even in disadvantaged communities. What we see taking place in neighborhood networking is more aligned with what Henry Jenkins (2006) calls the "participation gap," where it is no longer a matter of simply having the technology, but knowing what to do with it. Actively participating in a net locality means being privy to the rules. It means knowing the best way to connect with neighbors and to consult politicians. It means not just having access to a communication tool, but knowing how best to use it for political and social gain. The ability to cut, paste, and share online is a digital literacy with a wide range of competencies (Jenkins, 2006; Lenhart *et al.*, 2007), and how these competencies are used to mobilize and foster community is contingent on how well they are designed and supported by an existing social infrastructure.

Designing Engagement

There has been a flaw with many local engagement projects. Issues of accessibility, usability, and integration in everyday life in neighborhoods have been given inadequate attention. Context often gets left out of design decisions because it is commonly believed that the development of a platform for communication is enough to foster social and political engagement. However, for these projects to respond to the mounting criticism about inequality and usability, they need to factor in recruitment and group dynamics into the equation. Good and sustainable tools take time and coordination to build and execute.

As an example, a local engagement site in Scotland, called Digital Fife, addresses this problem head on. The site's organizers actively recruit and train users. They offer online tutorials in web design and physical world community-learning workshops to assist group organizers in using the tools. This pro-active measure of physically introducing the locality to the network has worked to increase the diversity and sustainability of participating neighborhoods.

The Neighbors for Neighbors (NFN) project in Boston, Massachusetts also adopts this advocacy approach. It is a platform for local neighborhood networking that launched in March 2008 to serve the needs of the Jamaica Plain neighborhood of the city. In 2009, in cooperation with the City of Boston, it was launched citywide. As of January 2010, the site claimed more than 2,600 registered users and more than 10,000 unique visits each month. NFN was started by the community activist Joseph Porcelli who says that he was inspired to create the digital network because "not everyone wanted to wear nametags" (personal interview, 2010). Porcelli is also responsible for the Nametag Project. In 2007, he wore a nametag everyday and passed out over 19,000 nametags throughout Boston so that people would feel more comfortable talking to their neighbors. "The project made an important point, but was not sustainable," he said. "Neighbors for Neighbors was my next step. The digital network was about getting people to talk to each other in real life without having to wear a nametag" (personal interview, 2010).

NFN was designed to facilitate group formation and civic action. It is not only organized by geographic boundaries, but by civic interest within the neighborhood. Groups formed based on safety, children, art, neighborhood walks, running, board games, and ultimate Frisbee (just to name a few), and have inspired physical meet-ups and civic action. For example, on September 24, 2009, there were three muggings in five hours on a particular street in Jamaica Plain. Porcelli sent a note to his neighborhood group and inspired hundreds of people to get out and flier the area to spread the word about the incidents. "For a week, people were having dinner on their front porches so that they could keep an eye on the street." And the incidents of crime on the street halted. Because something was posted online, people changed their behavior in the neighborhood.

NFN was effective for spreading information and giving people the opportunity to act on that information because it limited its demands on its users. The system was designed to require only intermittent attention from users – attention formulated from the concerns of physical communities and manifested in digital form. It could not work otherwise. People are beginning to complain about Facebook and Twitter burnout because they feel overwhelmed by the constant stream of data. In fact, in a June 2010 post on the official Facebook blog, the topic was "How to avoid social network burnout." Facebook users are struggling with the constant demands the system is putting on their lives. And net localities are adding to this. The systems that best take advantage of physical spaces coming online are ones that treat physical locations as yet another organizing structure of social life and attempt to fit them into accepted platforms for online interaction.

For example, the Virtual Birmingham Briefing Hub (b-scape) is a project out of the United Kingdom which worked with "virtual models" of the city to coordinate online interaction. It was a mash-up between the virtual world Second Life and Google Earth where avatars could walk through Google Earth within the Second Life environment. According to Birmingham city councilor Philip Mcgrahan, the project was designed to engage wider members of the public in consultation exercises, in particular where new urban developments are planned. The 2D and 3D maps of Birmingham's city center will allow planned builds to be showcased – permitting members of the public – both local and of the wider (Second Life) community – to comment on how the building fits in with the surrounding area and how they think it will enhance Birmingham (or otherwise).[6]

The goal of this project was to engage people in Birmingham's physical environment through the production of a virtual experience. More importantly, the goal was to encourage public deliberation over changes in the physical environment through the organized browsing of a virtual environment. "Wandering around Second Life demonstrates how natural it can be to build and explore 3D structures and environments through the medium of a human-shaped, human-acting avatar," says technologist Wade Roush. "Browsing Google Earth demonstrates what a sense of freedom and mastery comes from having tip-of-your-fingers access to an entire globe's worth of geographical data at multiple levels of resolution" (Roush, 2007). This kind of user experience has proven to be a useful tool for engaging people in urban space and civic issues. The Briefing Hub was constructed in order to connect people with their local environments. While traditionally virtual worlds have been considered spaces that disconnect users from their surrounding space, this experiment is actively repurposing virtual worlds to emphasize the connection to the local.

Although there have been claims that textual interfaces are actually more powerful in immersing users in another (virtual) space (Murray, 1999; Dibbell, 1999), it is clear that when it comes to enhancing the connection to existing physical spaces, a graphic interface can be very powerful. Navigating through a 3D design on a computer terminal can invite very strong connections to the space navigated. For example, the University of Victoria campus was reconstructed using the Unreal Tournament 2003 video game engine to help users visualize changes associated with campus construction (2005). While the user interface contained all the functionality of a first-person shooter game (with in-game weapons removed), the experience focused not on video game play, but rather on exploration and virtual mobility. Here the user is again challenged to forge links between physical and represented space.

Despite the fantasies of spontaneous eruptions of civic participation, the deliberate mobilization of net localities requires work. NFN, for example, relied on volunteer neighborhood captains to spark dialogue, and Porcelli spent much of his time coordinating with city employees and the police department to cull relevant information and participation. The Briefing Hub required the coordination with city planning offices and the organization of events where people gathered in the online space. While it is certainly possible to get widespread participation by simply setting up a platform (i-Neighbors demonstrates this), local, manual coordination is essential for maintaining and diversifying engagement in a local context (Gordon & Manosevitch, 2010).

Face-to-face interaction

Hub2, an interactive project by Eric Gordon and Gene Koo, took this one step further by connecting the experience of the space with the experience of face-to-face deliberation.[7] The core of the project was a series of community workshops, where residents gathered in a physical meeting space, each with a laptop. Participants interacted with one another both in the physical space of the room and the "virtual" space of the computer.

Hub2 took place in the summer of 2008 as part of the planning process associated with the construction of a neighborhood park. As a means of enhancing the traditional planning meeting where a few people assemble in a school gymnasium and look at a PowerPoint presentation, Hub2 sought to make this most local of events a more participatory experience. Everyone

Figure 5.1 Group of participants gathered at a Hub2 workshop in 2008, with the Second Life space in the foreground. Reproduced by permission of Engagement Game Lab.

that was present at the meeting was also present in Second Life. The meeting was run in such a way that the verbal conversation was integrated with activities in the virtual space. Participants used their avatars to move structures around, propose ideas for new structures and leave text comments. They also spoke with one another in the room to discuss their experience of "being in the park." For example, one participant said, "I could really feel the space. At first, I didn't, but then I did. It felt like I was really in the park, while another explained, "It's easier in Second Life to visualize the space. If you want to look at the streets, you can go over to them. If you just want to get an idea of an area, you can see a one-dimensional drawing, but if you want to immerse yourself, you use Second Life" (Gordon & Manosevitch, 2010). This project fostered an augmentation of the deliberation process, where people built on the correlations between what was happening in the virtual environment and what was happening in physical space, often using actions in the Second Life space as justifications for their proposals for the park.

Another project called Participatory Chinatown launched in spring 2010.[8] Guided by a similar desire to augment deliberation, this was a

Figure 5.2   Community members in Boston's Chinatown playing a game about their neighborhood called Participatory Chinatown. Photography by Nathaniel Hansen and Matthew Hashiguchi. Reproduced by permission of Matthew Hashiguchi.

game that used role-play to enhance a player's connection to their local space. It was made available to the community in a single player online version and a multiplayer version designed for the community meeting. At the live events, participants sat around one of five rectangular tables aligned with laptops networked together and all displaying the game. After a few introductory remarks, participants were instructed to pick a character from the selection screen. The player takes their assigned character and navigates the streets of Chinatown completing quests related to living, working, and socializing in the neighborhood. During this time, players were instructed to speak to each other and share resources both in and out of the game environment. The role-playing within the game forced the players to step outside of their idiosyncratic subject positions for a brief spell and respond to the neighborhood as someone different. It is well established that role-play in video games can lead to a more empathetic understanding of a social situation.[9] The goal was to transform this empathy into better decisions and better feed-back for urban planners. Players responded favorably to the game experience in general, and made specific mention of how meaningful it was to see their neighborhood from someone else's perspective. This foreign point-of-view informed their decisions in the remainder of the planning process and left a lasting impression of the experience. All player comments were made available for planners and city officials, and were posted online for general consumption and commentary.

Ultimately, what is unique about Hub2 and Participatory Chinatown is their emphasis on local, live engagement in addition to networked commentary and data access. Designing face-to-face engagement is expensive and labor intensive, but it directly responds to the critiques of inequity that are attached to many neighborhood networking projects. Participatory Chinatown, for instance, did not require participants to have high quality phones or computers to participate. The majority of engagement was facilitated in a physical space with technology on hand. It also did not require participants to speak English. In addition to having interpreters in the room, the game's text was translated into Chinese.

These projects demonstrate the importance of designing for the context of physical interaction. While they took advantage of networked information, role-play, and immersive visualizations, the ultimate goal was to create meaningful experiences based in, and organized around, physical location. Especially as individual data accessibility and connectivity grows increasingly robust, attention to low-tech concerns such as face-to-face talk is too often overlooked.

Hyperlocal News

Community involvement in local issues does not only exist in the form of neighborhood forums and online social environments. The ability to directly communicate with each other via the web and mobile devices not only makes people more aware of what is happening in their local communities, but also radically inverts the established model of news production and distribution. Traditional journalism has been developed as a top-down system in which news was crafted by a small number of newspapers and distributed to the population. But the ease of uploading local information to the web gives people the power to produce news about their neighborhoods, therefore contributing to a stronger awareness of their local spaces.

In Nicholas Negroponte's 1995 book *Being Digital,* he prophesized the end of the daily newspaper as it is replaced by the "daily me," or a fully customizable stream of digital information.[10] News stories can be updated within seconds online without the need to wait for tomorrow's edition. And instead of browsing through an editor's opinion of "top stories" through various RSS readers or even newspaper websites, users can filter stories to their specific interests. Whether it is technology, business, Chinese politics, or geographic location, the user is capable of constructing their own editorial voice based on any number of filters. Clay Shirky (2008) argues that news has moved from a "filter, then publish," model to a "publish, then filter" model. Filtering becomes part of the act of consumption.

This dynamic is interestingly reflected in recent transformations in the newspaper business. The traditional newspaper model employs a one-size fits all format organized around a geographic location (a city or country) that is, in the contemporary personalized marketplace, too big to be meaningful. The job of each city newspaper has been to publish local, national, and international stories. But as all news content is freely available online, a national story in the *Kansas City Star* is no more relevant to a Kansas City resident than a national story in the *New York Times*. And, considering the resources of news desks at most newspapers, the *New York Times* article is likely to be better. So, what is a newspaper in a medium sized city to do? The answer is to focus on the content that the *New York Times* or political bloggers whose content feeds into Google News, cannot focus on: local content. As national and international news desks at small and medium-sized city newspapers are compressing, newspapers are turning to the "hyperlocal" – news localization on the street or neighborhood scale, not the city or national scale. Newspapers' approach to exploiting the hyperlocal is to claim a stake in the machine aggregation of content. Location is the one category for which authority is necessarily localized.

But that does not mean authority is assigned to traditional journalists. Much to the dismay of local news desks, local bloggers have been better at hyperlocal coverage (Farhi, 2007). The *Los Angeles Times*, for instance, has always had a Metro section, but it does not have the staff or the funding to meet the needs of every neighborhood. The person looking for news about the local shop owner will likely not find what they are looking for. On the other hand, a person living next to the shop, who perhaps knows from personal interaction with the owner, why the business has shuttered after only three months, will have a great deal more to say.

As an example, Baristanet covers the New York suburbs of Montclair and Bloomsfield, New Jersey, and is comprised of a steady stream of local news tidbits. The co-founder, Debbie Galant, said of the site, "we differ from the local newspaper in point of view: we have one" (Williams, 2005). By 2007, this point of view had attracted more than 80,000 unique visitors a month, resulting in a steady income stream from local advertisers. Or consider

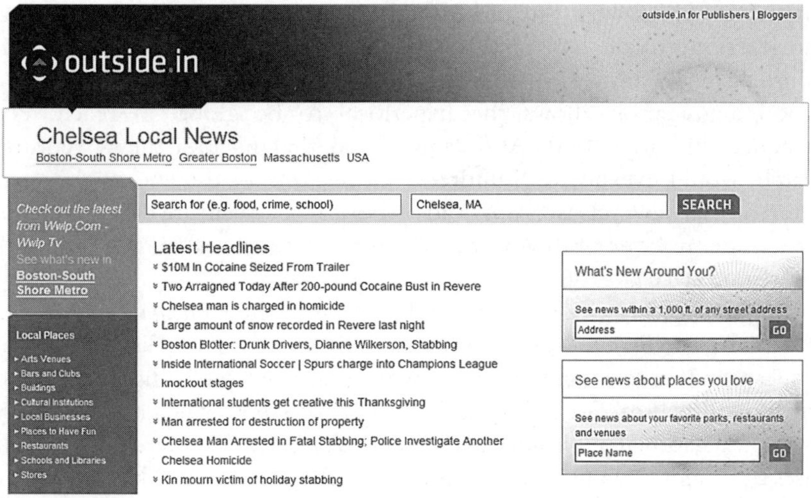

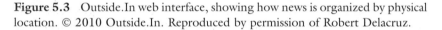

Figure 5.3 Outside.In web interface, showing how news is organized by physical location. © 2010 Outside.In. Reproduced by permission of Robert Delacruz.

Fresno Famous, a local blog from Fresno, California, that was so successful, it was purchased by the city's major newspaper, the *Fresno Bee*. There is clearly value in the local.

This desire for local content is nothing new. Neighborhood newspapers have long provided a reliable business model – local advertisers and local readers. But blogs have raised the stakes of local coverage, because they have been able to converge the consumption of local information with the production of local information. When local newspapers failed to cover something, people took it upon themselves to cover it.

The site Outside.in has taken advantage of this. The hyperlocal content and advertising platform is a very simple application. One need only type in a zip code or address and the system will spit back relevant blog entries. Its innovation is its simplicity – and its business model. As of January 2010, Outside.in serviced 57,830 neighborhoods. For most users, the service is free. The company makes its money in packaging and delivering that localized content to mainstream media organizations. In December 2009, it announced that it would be supplying local news feeds to CNN's website and earned a corresponding infusion of $7 million in venture funding, bringing the company's total to $12 million. This was possibly a response to the August 2009 sale of the local news aggregator EveryBlock to MSNBC. It was in 2009 that hyperlocal news became big business. And not unexpectedly, it is also the year that several small, hyperlocal blogs went out of business. As John Smith said: "It's a para-doxical notion, one that seems to strike at the whole notion of 'hyperlocal' journalism: To stay very small, you may have to get very big" (Farhi, 2007). Local aggregation allows the hyperlocal to be global in reach. For instance, in early 2010, AOL announced that its local news venture, Patch, would expand to "hundreds" of markets by the end of the year. In an official news release, AOL said of its local news venture that it wants to be a leader in "one of the most promising 'white spaces' on the Internet" (Carlson, 2010).

Regional or big city newspapers, for instance the *Chicago Tribune*, the *LA Times*, the *Boston Globe*, and the *New York Times* have taken this lesson to heart and are seeking to fill in that white space by capitalizing on local and citizen journalism. For example, the *New York Times*, which has ostensibly become a national publication, launched "The Local" in March of 2009. It uses the tagline: "Your town. Your neighborhood. Your block. Covered by you" and covers five New York-area neighborhoods. The idea aspires to combine efforts of full-time *Times* journalists and "citizen journalists" to create a local site with local flavor, while not sacrificing the benefits of big newspaper affiliation, including access to institutions and events. The site has daily updates, stories reported by local people about local concerns, and through the guidance of professional reporters, it seeks to maintain the journalistic standards of the *Times*. In addition to news reporting, there are forums for parents, calendars for events, and bulletin boards for death notices. It is meant to capture the concerns of the local neighborhood, while maintaining the prestige and visibility of a big city newspaper. By capturing local readers motivated by local content, the *Times* is essentially strengthening its national brand through its representation of the local.[11]

Government 2.0

As large-scale newspapers are seeking to follow the model of hyperlocal journalism to recover the connection with local communities, local gov-ernments are also struggling to find their role in this. City governments, especially in the United States and Europe, are seeking to engage their citizens at a time when public engagement is increasingly happening outside the reach of government. While the government continues to control the city's parks and recreation areas, most other spaces, especially as they become networked, are operating in a public fashion without the official public stamp of government. Net localities are forcing governments to evaluate the role they play in "public" life.

It is nothing particularly new for local governments to have a web presence and even to have certain services (like paying parking tickets and taxes) available online. But there is growing pressure for them to incorporate more meaningful participation into those services in order to play a role in facilitating public (and perhaps even democratic) dialogue. In what is commonly referred to as Government 2.0 (Bain, 2008), social network sites (SNS), wikis, and mobile applications are brought to bear on government services. There is ample evidence that web presence increases opportunities for meaningful engagement in local life (Hampton & Wellman, 2003; Urry, 2003). As such, city governments are struggling with how to engage a networked population. People expect different kinds of access to services and information. Even as more and more local information is discoverable through the web, the information that falls within the purview of government, such as taxes and property lines, school services, transportation routes, and so on, is too often inaccessible. Governments are slow to adopt these tools primarily because they fear the corresponding data transparency that accompanies net locality. Not only does it potentially threaten individual privacy, but it also challenges the ability for government to operate without constant scrutiny. While some scholars celebrate the possibility of openness with government data (Noveck, 2008), suggesting that scrutiny is essential for democracy, others question the positive correlation between democracy and data transparency (Lessig, 2009), arguing that scrutiny based on incomplete data sources can sometimes lead to chaos. But, in spite of the efficacy of transparency, governments are confronted with a much bigger issue: the expectations of their constituents. Many people have come to expect a certain kind of access to data and ability to participate. As such, big city (and some small town) governments have incorporated social networking and data access into their list of essential services, competing with one another over their ability to embrace "innovation" and "openness."

In October 2009, *Next American City Magazine* in partnership with the Rockefeller Foundation staged a conference in Washington, DC called "Open Cities: New Media's Role in Shaping Urban Policy." At the event, speakers ranged from city officials to technology entrepreneurs to members of the Obama administration. The primary theme of the two-day event was openness in government data. The conference focused on building coalitions between technologists and city governments, with the general bias toward the idea that more data equals better citizenship. When public data, including tax records, housing assessments, locations of city-planted trees, crime and transportation data is not only accessible, but easily distributed in common file formats, the possibilities are endless. Just in

2009, the governments of the United States, Britain, New Zealand and Australia have all prioritized the release of machine-readable data for public appropriation. Even to the extent that this data existed at the time, it had created a rush on iPhone applications for granting locally contextualized access to city data. For example, iTransitBuddy provides GPS locations for city buses in metro areas such as Chicago, Denver, Long Island, and Philadelphia; iCommuteSF and iBART Live do the same for San Francisco; Citizens Connect is a location-based city hotline in Boston; and New York City has at least a dozen applications for transportation as well as NYC311 for citizen complaints.

These applications use the GPS feature on location-aware phones to contextualize city data to the location of the user. Whether it is looking for the best bike paths, seeing crime statistics, charting the location of a bus, or reporting a pothole, these tools move several steps beyond the non-contextual transit authority websites or city sites. Being able to identify city services or submit complaints that are specific to the user's local context shifts the user experience from one of active searching to letting oneself be searched. In other words, these applications provide the impression that simply being in a place is the first step toward interacting with urban data and therefore engaging with the city.

This is a valuable impression. Making the city user-friendly has been a goal of architects and planners for decades (Gordon, 2010). Walkable streets, clear transportation routes, and government responsiveness: these goals are nothing new. Urban design has long been central to feelings of engagement. The question is, can the digital design of urban data, and the subsequent personalization of the city's interface, have an effect on one's feeling of belonging to a place or engaging with the civic life of a city? Or is the focus on these tools, as some claim, merely a distraction from the day-to-day problems of city governance? For example, in a letter to the *Boston Globe* about the city's Citizens Connect application, Lisa McDonough writes:

> It is funny to see this trumpeted as the best thing ever, and although I agree that it is a powerful tool, once the city considers itself "deluged" again, the exact same logjam will occur. If it happened with the older technology why would it not happen again once more people adopt the new one? The City of Boston needs a complete attitude change, and that change needs to extend to people who use any form of technology, or for that matter even old-fashioned mail. (McDonough, 2010)

McDonough's complaint is that the city is mistaking the new for the good; she suggests that other, more traditional problems of urbanism and governance should take precedence over the introduction of new tools. Other arguments against such services focus on inequality. In reference to Government 2.0 initiatives in general, the blogger Joshua Allen (2010) asks the following questions: "Are we really comfortable with a system that gives privileged treatment to people who can afford data plans and GPS-enabled devices? Have we become so isolated from real people, that we gullibly accept that Craig Newmark [of Craig's List] represents the common man?"

Government 2.0 efforts are plagued with the problems of exclusion (which we will discuss in detail in Chapter 6). Only, with government, personal exclusionary practices are potentially authenticated through policy. Building infrastructure that only some people can access might not truly be public infrastructure. But this is like saying that building a bridge, when not everyone has a car, is not truly public infrastructure. The bridge alleviates traffic and organizes transportation patterns in the city. Even for those without a car, the bridge likely will yield a demonstrable effect. The same is true for an iPhone application that facilitates real time, locally situated communication with a government office. Not everyone possesses the hardware or the knowledge to communicate, but like the bridge, its existence becomes one of many tools to facilitate urban flow. Different from a bridge, however, the flexibility of the media and the relatively inexpensive and rapid development processes enable cities to adopt these tools without excluding other, more available forms of communication (like websites or telephone hotlines). In addition, cities are increasingly investing in education and outreach to get people involved and in some cases giving people access to the technologies needed to participate. Despite this, spending limited resources on what some see as boutique digital tools remains a politically risky venture.

Perhaps this is why many government tools have been developed by third-parties seeking to form partnerships with government. The UK-based FixMyStreet, for example, is a reporting tool (website and iPhone app) that allows users to report problems in any city in the United Kingdom and Canada. When someone reports graffiti or a pothole, the site generates a report and sends it to the relevant city agency. The agencies are urged to respond by taking action and updating the status of the complaint on the website. By the end of 2009, there were over 68,000 reports generated or commented on in the United Kingdom alone. These are impressive numbers that demonstrate the usefulness of such tools. However, problems have emerged with its success. There are an increasing amount of ignored reports as their number becomes too large for government agencies to handle. The success of these tools is mitigated by the capacity of the institutions in place to handle increased levels of participation. And as capacity building focuses on responding to this new stream of inputs, concern rises about the already limited resources of government offices being shifted to accommodate them.

SeeClickFix is a US-based company that offers similar services. Users report problems, see other problems reported, and follow or subscribe to certain issues or communities. Like FixMyStreet, SeeClickFix generates reports and sends them to the appropriate city agency. Unlike FixMyStreet, SeeClickFix has taken some important measures to address the problems of engagement identified above. In attempting to convince people that this one-size-fits-all tool is appropriate to their locality, they seek citizen volunteers, or what they call "sideclicks" to function as ambassadors to local municipalities. By getting local people to usher in the use of the service, by promoting the tool in local meetings, communicating personally with local officials, and staying in touch with the company to provide feedback on the service, they are attempting to mitigate the anxiety associated with many local government tools – that the local is being filtered through a global network. In addition to this, SeeClickFix is addressing the issue of sustained interest. One of the problems with these tools is that few provide motivation to participate outside of the desire to do good or the immediate need for information. SeeClickFix has adopted game elements, in the form of "civic points," to promote sustained interest. Users earn points by registering for the site, reporting an issue, getting others to comment on their issue, uploading videos, logging in seven days in a row, and getting a problem fixed. The point system is intended to provide competition as an incentive to participate, with the top civic point-earners in each city prominently displayed. This game-like quality of the site seeks to transform the day-to-day drudgery of civic engagement into something playful, tied to social networks, and most of all, convenient (Kahne, Middaugh, & Evans, 2008). This blurring of civic tools and games is similar to the blurring we discussed in Chapter 3 between social networks and games. Game elements are being implemented to provide incentive to participate, even though the application itself cannot be wholly characterized as a game.

Net localities are becoming operationalized in cities through the kind of public/private partnership we see in the examples above. The kind of innovative approaches to participation that are seen in SeeClickFix would likely not emerge out of a city technology office. Spending city dollars on a game, for instance, is not yet politically palatable. The public sector is stodgier than the private sector (Hansell, 2009). Civic governance is often driven by a no-fail and steady progress ethos, while the private sector is more likely to take chances on a new idea. The role of government, in this regard, is about providing the raw materials from which to build. This is reflected in Barack Obama's "Transparency and Open Government" memo (2009). In it he placed a priority on transparency, ordering most government offices to make their data available on http://data.gov, the federal government's catalog of machine-readable data. Similarly, the United Kingdom has launched http://data.gov.uk for the same purpose. In addition to just making this data available, government agencies in the United States and the United Kingdom have held competitions for local developers to use the newly available data (*Economist*, 2010).

Governments are realizing the benefits of outsourcing citizen engagement, as the development of new tools associated with this age-old practice require rather specialized expertise. Some of the most prominent examples include Washington, DC's "Apps for Democracy," where, in 2008, the city partnered with a firm called iStrategyLabs to launch a competition for using government data.[12] In one year, $50,000 in prize money produced 47 iPhone and Facebook applications. Similar competitions are being held also in traditionally very conservative sectors as well. For instance, the Defense Advanced Research Projects Agency (DARPA) in the United States has released much of its data for an application competition.

As this deluge of data reaches the average web or smart phone user, other challenges emerge that have to do with coordination of users and agencies and the interoperability of redundant applications. There is perhaps such a thing as too much of a good thing when it comes to data accessibility. This data excess and the problems associated with it are indicative of net localities, where the presence of data and the expectations of its accessibility are limited only by the available network signal and the hardware one carries. Some have referred to this new urban subject as "Citizen 2.0" (Drapeau, 2010), an adaptation of citizens to Government 2.0 and net locality more generally. In this flurry of new data sets and applications to read them, government has to reconsider its role in engaging people. It has to move beyond what Donald Kettl (2009) has called "vending machine government," where the full body of services is determined beforehand, and toward what Tim O'Reilly (2009) has called "government as platform," where citizens contribute to identifying and solving issues.

According to O'Reilly, government should be an open platform, which allows people inside and outside of government to contribute to an ever-growing ecosystem of innovation. He compares this vision of government to the kind of ecosystem Apple was able to establish in iTunes. There is a lucrative business model for being the platform and there is considerable incentive for people to use the platform. According to O'Reilly:

> Rather than licensing government data to a few select "value added" providers, who then license the data downstream, the federal government

(and many state and local governments) are beginning to provide an open platform that enables anyone with a good idea to build innovative services that connect government to citizens, give citizens visibility into the actions of government and even allow citizens to participate directly in policy-making. (O'Reilly, 2009)

The government as platform model is quite promising in that it is designed to accommodate the expectations of its constituents. However, the most challenging aspect of this new model of governance will be the maintenance of interoperability and flexibility in the system. If some of these tools fail to work together, if there is too much redundancy, the whole system will shut down. And there is nothing worse than a platform full of bugs, especially one to which you pay taxes.

The Politics of Net Localities

Whether it is facilitated by citizens or by the government, the presence of digital networks in local life is changing the nature of local communities. What it looks and feels like to "know your neighbors" is altered in net localities. Elements of Gemeinschaft, or local, ritualized correspondence, are blending with the algorithmic community formations that have become familiar in SNS. Talking to neighbors can happen on a front porch, at a community meeting, a protest, or in a chat room. Likewise, what it means to participate in politics is altered in net localities. Reporting a pothole with SeeClickFix is participation, sharing information on Neighbors for Neighbors is participation, playing a game about a local planning initiative is participation, and certainly, rallying in a public square is participation. The platforms from which to participate are proliferating, to the point where local participation in politics is blurring with participation more generally in net localities. Sharing, commenting and organizing are what people do online. That those activities have implications for our geographical communities is the inevitable result of a population that is location aware.

As a consequence, governments find themselves in an interesting bind. They must govern net localities in order to stay relevant; but they also must realize the inequities of these spaces in order to remain effective. And yet, this dilemma is hardly slowing down the public sector's enthusiasm for bringing new tools to bear on government and engagement. Nearly every large city in the United States and Europe is putting some effort into cultivating net localities, by building tools or by engaging with existing local networks. Government is no longer about simply managing public life; it is about providing a public platform for interaction between people and local data.

But the popularity of online social platforms and location-aware applications to interact with local communities and public spaces leads to increased fears about the loss of privacy and control over personal spaces. These issues will be addressed in Chapter 6.

Notes

1 But this is not true for everyone. Engagement among African American and working class youth, for example, continues to be on the decline. This is what they refer to as the "post-9/11 split."

2 See Carr, 2010 and Lanier, 2010 for arguments on the negative social influences of digital communication; for positive influences on political and social life, see Jenkins, 2006; Kahne, Middaugh, & Evans, 2008; Shirky, 2008.

3 While early online virtual worlds created community by anonymity (i.e., users did not typically disclose their identities and they interacted with others via digital personas, aka avatars), social networking sites (SNS) are built on the premise that people are who they say they are. And this happens because connections on SNS normally reflect pre-existing social ties. As Boyd and Ellison (2007) noted, social relationships on SNS originate offline and are transferred online. This is the opposite of the online virtual world model, in which new online connections developed, and these connections could eventually be transferred offline.

4 For examples of neighborhood communication, see Hampton & Wellman, 2003; Hampton, 2007; Kavanaugh *et al.*, 2005.

5 The field of social network analysis has demonstrated that weak ties within neighborhoods, rather than leading to social isolation, provide the foundation for strong communities. Keith Hampton (2007) points out that this sort of social network has shown to provide significant community benefits such as help with home improvements and emergency child care (Wellman & Wortley, 1990, pp. 569–570). It has also demonstrated to lead to lower crime rates (Sampson & Groves, 1989), and reduced mental distress (Elliott, 2000; Ross, 2000).

6 Personal correspondence with Gordon, 2010.

7 For more details about this project, see Foth *et al.*, 2009; Gordon & Koo, 2008; Gordon & Manosevitch, 2010.

8 Participatory Chinatown was funded by the MacArthur Foundation and it was a collaborative effort between three Boston-area organizations: Emerson College, the Asian Community Development Corporation, and the Metropolitan Area Planning Council.

9 For research on empathy, see DeNeve & Heppner, 1997; Simkins & Steinkuehler, 2008; Yee & Bailenson, 2006.

10   Of course, he was not solely enthusiastic about the possibility. Apart from the devastating effect it would have on the medium of newsprint, he warned of the effects on the consumer. The hyper-personalization of information, he lamented, could lead to homeostasis, essentially narrowing the field of information for each individual just as the amount of accessible data continued to grow. Others have echoed this concern (Johnson, 2001) and introduced the implications of a positive feedback loop that we see demonstrated in popular consumer services such as Amazon Recommended for You (Sunstein, 2006), where your decisions from yesterday determine what you see today.

11   These local efforts would seem to be good for the neighborhoods they serve, but they have not been without criticism. In response to the Local's initial blog post, one reader named "clintonhiller" said the following: "While I am happy that you are touting the merits of my neighborhood (I moved in a year ago from Manhattan) I am concerned that this cutesy blog will make the neighborhood more popular and subsequently price me out of it as has happened to me with other neighborhood (sic). There are plenty of blogs already about Brooklyn and this neighborhood. There is no need to mass-produce a blog that will do nothing but raise rents, change the businesses and people who frequent them and actually ruin the neighborhood you're trying to promote. Keep promoting the West Village as cute and quirky and the East Village as grungy. Let us keep our neighborhood as is." The concern that local bloggers could bring unwanted attention to a locality is quite prevalent in reactions to similar ventures (Lindgren, 2009). If local reporting brings positive attention to a neighborhood, it just might increase property values. Navigating community needs for privacy and the desire for publicity is one of the biggest challenges facing newspapers' rapid ascent into the hyperlocal.

12   The Chief Technology Officer (CTO) of DC was a man named Vivek Kundra, who was appointed the CTO in the Obama Administration.

References

Allen, J. (2010, January 11). Government 2.0: Activist paradise, or treading on the poor? *Mix Online*. Retrieved November 1, 2010 from http://visitmix.com/opinions/Government-20-Activist-Hero-or-Treading-on-the-Poor

Bain, B. (2008, March 20). Tapscott: Governance by participation. *Federal Computer Week*. Retrieved November 1, 2010 from http://www.fcw.com/print/22_6/features/151973-1.html

Boyd, D. M., & Ellison, N. B. (2007). Social network sites: Definition, history, and scholarship. *Journal of Computer-Mediated Communication, 13*(1), article 11. Retrieved November 1, 2010 from http://jcmc.indiana.edu/vol13/issue1/boyd.ellison.html

Carlson, N. (2010, February 17). AOL to launch "hundreds" of local news sites in 2010. *Business Insider*. Retrieved November 1, 2010 from http://www

.businessinsider.com/aol-plans-to-launch-hundreds-of-local-news-sites-in
-2010-2010-2

Carr, N. (2010). *The shallows: What the Internet is doing to our brains.* New York: W.W. Norton.

Castells, M. (2009). *Communication power.* Oxford and New York: Oxford University Press.

DeNeve, K. M., & Heppner, M. J. (1997). Role play simulations: The assessment of an active learning technique and comparisons with traditional lectures. *Innovative Higher Education, 21*(3), 231–246.

Dibbell, J. (1999). *My tiny life: Crime and passion in a virtual world.* New York: Henry Holt.

Drapeau, M. (2010, January 8). Government 2.0, meet Citizen 2.0. *Federal Computer Week.* Retrieved November 1, 2010 from http://fcw.com/articles/2010/01/11/comment-drapeau-government-20.aspx

Economist. (2010, February 4). Of governments and geeks. *The Economist.* Retrieved November 1, 2010 from http://www.economist.com/node/15469415?story_id=15469415

Elliott, M. (2000). The stress process in neighborhood context. *Health and Place, 6*(4), 287–299.

Engagement Game Lab. (2009–10). Participatory Chinatown [Game]. Retrieved November 1, 2010 from http://engagementgamelab.org

Farhi, P. (2007). Rolling the dice. *American Journalism Review,* June/July. Retrieved November 1, 2010 from http://www.ajr.org/article.asp?id=4343

Foth, M., Bajracharya, B., Brown, R., & Hearn, G. (2009). The second life of urban planning? Using neogeography tools for community engagement. *Journal of Location Based Services, 3*(2), 97–117.

Gordon, E. (2010). *The urban spectator: American concept-cities from Kodak to Google.* Hanover, NH: Dartmouth College Press.

Gordon, E., & Koo, G. (2008). Placeworlds: Using virtual worlds to foster civic engagement. *Space and Culture, 11*(3), 204–221.

Gordon, E., & Manosevitch, E. (2010, June 21). Augmented deliberation: Merging physical and virtual interaction to engage communities in urban planning. *New Media & Society.* DOI:10.1177/1461444810365315

Hampton, K. N. (2007). Neighborhoods in the network society the e-neighbors study. *Information, Communication & Society, 10*(5), 714–748.

Hampton, K. N. (2010). Internet use and the concentration of disadvantage: Glocalization and the urban underclass. *American Behavioral Scientist, 53*(8), 1111–1132.

Hampton, K., & Wellman, B. (2003). Neighboring in Netville: How the internet supports community and social capital in a wired suburb. *City and Community, 2*(4), 277–311.

Hansell, S. (2009, March 17). Government 2.0 meets catch 22 [Blog post]. Retrieved November 1, 2010 from http://bits.blogs.nytimes.com/2009/03/17/government-20-meets-catch-22/

Jeffres, L.W. (2008). An urban communication audit: Measuring aspects of a communicative city. *Gazette, 70,* 257–273.

Jenkins, H. (2006). *Convergence culture: Where old and new media collide.* New York: New York University Press.

Johnson, S. (2001). Emergence: The connected lives of ants, brains, cities and software. New York: Scribner.

Kahlenberg, R. R. (2005, April 30). Social network blossoms in well-linked neighborhood. *Washington Post.* Retrieved November 1, 2010 from http://www.washingtonpost.com/wp-dyn/content/article/2005/04/29/AR2005042900657.html

Kahne, J., Middaugh, E., & Evans, C. (2008). *The civic potential of video games* [White Paper]. MacArthur Foundation. Retrieved November 1, 2010 from http://www.civicsurvey.org/Civic_Potential_of_Games.pdf

Kapor, M. (1993). Where is the digital highway really heading? *Wired Magazine.* Retrieved November 1, 2010 from http://wired.com/wired/archive/1.03/kapor.on.nii_pr.html

Katz, J., & Aahkus, M. (2002). *Perpetual contact: Mobile communication, private talk, public performance.* Cambridge: Cambridge University Press.

Kavanaugh, A., Isenhour, P., Cooper, M., Carroll, J. M., Rosson, M. B., & Schmitz, J. (2005). Information technology in support of public deliberation. In van den Besselaar, P., de Michelis, G., Preece J., & Simone, C. (Eds.). *Communities and Technologies* (pp. 19–40). The Netherlands: Kluwer Academic.

Kettl, D. (2009). *The next government of the United States: Why our institutions fail us and how to fix them.* New York: W.W. Norton.

Lanier, J. (2010). *You are not a gadget: A manifesto.* New York: Knopf.

Lenhart, A., Madden, M., Macgill, A. R., & Smith, A. (2007). *Teens and social media: The use of social media gains a greater foothold in teen life as they embrace the conversational nature of interactive online media.* Washington, DC: Pew Internet & American Life Project.

Lessig, L. (2009, October 9). Against transparency: The perils of openness in government. *The New Republic.* Retrieved November 1, 2010 from http://www.tnr.com/article/books-and-arts/against-transparency

Lindgren, T. (2009). Place blogging: Local economies of attention in the network. PhD dissertation, Boston College. Retrieved November 1, 2010 from www.placeblogging.com/

McDonough, L. (2010, February 8). Send photo, get action – for now. *The Boston Globe.* Retrieved November 1, 2010 from http://www.boston.com/bostonglobe/editorial_opinion/letters/articles/2010/02/08/send_photo_get_action_for_now/

Meyrowitz, J. (1985). *No sense of place: the impact of electronic media on social behavior.* New York: Oxford University Press.

Moores, S. (2004). The doubling of place: electronic media, time-space arrangements and social relationships. In Couldry, B. & McCarthy, A. (Eds.), *Media/space: Place, scale and culture in a media age* (pp. 21). London: Routledge (Comedia).

Murray, J. (1999). *Hamlet on the Holodeck: The future of narrative in cyberspace.* Cambridge, MA: MIT Press.

Noveck, B. S. (2008). Wiki government: How open-source technology can make government decision-making more expert and more democratic. *Democracy Journal, 7* (Winter). Retrieved November 1, 2010 from http://www.democracyjournal.org/article.php?ID=6570

O'Reilly, T. (2009, August 10). Gov 2.0: The promise of innovation. *Forbes.com.* Retrieved November 1, 2010 from http://www.forbes.com/2009/08/10/government-internet-software-technology-breakthroughs-oreilly.html

Obama, B. (2009). Transparency and open government. *The Whitehouse.* Retrieved November 1, 2010 from http://www.whitehouse.gov/the_press_office/TransparencyandOpenGovernment/

Park, R., McKenzie, R. D., & Burgess, E. (1925). *The city: Suggestions for the study of human nature in the urban environment.* Chicago, IL: University of Chicago Press.

Plant, S. (2001, October 28). On the mobile. The effects of mobile telephones on social and individual life. *Motorola.* Excerpt retrieved November 1, 2010 from http://www.cyborganthropology.com/On_the_Mobile

Putnam, R. D. (2000). Bowling alone: The collapse and revival of American. *Community.* New York: Simon & Schuster.

Ross, C. E. (2000). Neighborhood disadvantage and adult depression. *Journal of Health and Social Behavior, 41*(2), 177–187.

Roush, W. (2007, September 18). My speech in second life: Moshing with metaverse-molders. *Xconomy.* Retrieved November 1, 2010 from http://www.xconomy.com/2007/09/18/moshing-with-metaverse-molders-in-second-life/

Sampson, R., & Groves, B. (1989). Community structure and crime: Testing social-disorganization theory. *American Journal of Sociology, 94*(4), 774–802.

Sander, T. H., & Putnam, R. D. (2010). Still bowling alone? The post-9/11 split. *Journal of Democracy, 21*(1), 9–16.

Shirky, C. (2008). *Here comes everybody: The power of organizing without organization.* New York: Penguin.

Simkins, D. W., & Steinkuehler, C. (2008). Critical ethical reasoning and role-play. *Games and Culture, 3*(3/4), 333–355.

Simmel, G. (1971). The metropolis and mental life. In *On individuality and social forms: selected writings.* Chicago, IL: University of Chicago Press.

Spigel, L. (1992). *Make room for TV: Television and the family ideal in postwar America.* Chicago, IL: University of Chicago Press.

Sunstein, C. (2006). *Infotopia: How many minds produce knowledge.* Oxford: Oxford University Press.

Tönnies, F. (2002). *Community and society.* New York: Dover.

Urry, J. (2003). Social networks, travel and talk. *British Journal of Sociology, 54*(2), 155–175.

Wellman, B., & Wortlet, S. (1990). Different strokes from different folks: Community ties and social support. *American Journal of Sociology, 96,* 558–588.

Williams, L. (2005). *If I didn't build it, they wouldn't come: Citizen journalism is discovered (alive) in Watertown, MA.* Retrieved November 1, 2010 from http://journalism.nyu.edu/pubzone/weblogs/pressthink/2005/11/14/lw _h2tn.html

Yee, N., & Bailenson, J. N. (2006). Walk a mile in digital shoes: The impact of embodied perspective-taking on the reduction of negative stereotyping in immersive virtual environments. Paper presented at PRESENCE 2006: The 9th Annual International Workshop on Presence, Cleveland, Ohio.

6

Privacy

Net locality cultivates a mastering of one's position in the network, but it also provides the conditions for one to be mastered *by* the network. The two sides of the coin are never separated. As we become more comfortable with the ubiquity of networks in our lives, we become less comfortable with being disconnected. Leaving the house without a mobile phone, or getting in the car without a GPS device might cause feelings of anxiety because it suggests a momentary disconnect from the network. This is what Mark Adrejevic (2007) called the "digital enclosure." Net localities are the physical manifestations of this enclosure.

The emergence of net localities marks a shift in the way we understand the web: from a digital network that operated outside the physical constraints of the world to one that exists in the spaces of everyday life, organized around physical location. In previous chapters, we have placed considerable emphasis on the social benefits of this shift – but there are costs as well. As physical location becomes an essential dataset for the construction and maintenance of digital networks, questions pertaining to the control and access to that data are taking center stage; specifically, how privacy, surveillance, control, and access are shaping urban spaces.

The disclosure of personal location information is necessary for location-aware applications, such as the ones in maps and mobile devices, to work. To take advantage of location data, people must be willing to share that information. However, even for those who enjoy the affordances of net locality, there is typically an accompanying anxiety with this form of personal disclosure. The act of making one's location information public is often accompanied by dystopian Orwellian fantasies of total surveillance.

Net Locality: Why Location Matters in a Networked World, First Edition. Eric Gordon and Adriana de Souza e Silva. © 2011 Eric Gordon and Adriana de Souza e Silva. Published 2011 by Blackwell Publishing Ltd.

Who knows who might be paying attention to where you are? But traditional metaphors of top-down surveillance are no longer adequate to address net localities, because the fashion in which people are surveilled and in which they surveil others is rather circular in orientation. Disclosing one's personal location does compromise one's control over the use of their data; however, it also opens up the possibilities of controlling data to fortify the functionality of one's location. In other words, location-aware technologies enable users to exclude people and information that are not immediately relevant to their situation. So while the fear of outside intrusion upon personal space and information threatens to remove personal control in public spaces, the increased capacity for personal control over physical space through information filtering presents other problems associated with social exclusion (de Souza e Silva & Frith, 2010a). The increased personalization of space introduced by new technologies suggests new kinds of exclusionary practices and shifts in power relationships that might challenge how spaces are experienced and who has access to those experiences.

This is the paradox of net locality – a personalized relationship to physical location that at the same time threatens and secures one's control of physical space. Although the borders between public and private spaces have constantly shifted throughout human history and although the development of each new transportation and communication technology has contributed to challenging these established borders, current location-aware technologies challenge us to question the traditional borders between what is considered public and what has been considered private. They also urge us to reconsider how we understand surveillance and power in society. As such, we witness a perceived invasion of privacy by the public disclosure of personal information, and simultaneously an attempt to "privatize" public spaces via the personal control over the information one can access about that space.

Fears of losing privacy originate from a concern about losing control of one's personal location information. These fears are associated with a traditional understanding of surveillance as a top-down form of power (exerted by the government, corporations, and unknown entities) intruding upon one's private space. In this chapter, we analyze these fears in the context of net localities, and argue for a different way of understanding surveillance and privacy. We also look at the way this new understanding is affecting the sorts of spaces described in Chapters 4 and 5. By using location-aware technologies, users command control over information flows in physical space. While this leads to new practices of urban spaces, it can also lead to exclusionary practices and the subsequent privatization of urban spaces. Ultimately, it all comes down to control – who gets to control our personal location data, and how we control the data of the locations we occupy.

The Public Nature of Location Data

Our whole world is becoming mapped. Initiatives like Google Maps and Google Street View are reminders that the surveillance of the world is extensive and that most consumers have achieved a certain amount of comfort with that surveillance. But Google has not been without its fair share of lawsuits. From the beginning of Google Maps, the company has had a policy in place to help facilitate the removal of photographs of one's person or property. So when San Francisco resident and Electronic Frontier Foundation (EFF) privacy advocate Kevin Bankston asked that his picture be removed from a street corner, Google replied with a request for his name, location of image, and copy of his driver's license. But Bankston was incensed by this demand: "Apparently, you have to jump through more hoops than a trained seal," he complained. "Perhaps they'd also like my mother's maiden name? Birth certificate? Urine sample?" (Poulsen, 2007). As a result of Bankston's protests, Google changed its policy, replacing the requirement of the driver's license with a signed statement of accuracy. The change in this policy resulted almost immediately in a windfall of new requests. People were generally unhappy with being part of the tacit public record. But most legal challenges have passed without incident for the company because privacy laws in the United States do not protect against being photographed in public space. Since all of Google's photographs were taken from public streets, the company is technically within their legal rights. However, the plans to expand to other countries have been interrupted by stricter privacy laws. Several European countries have denied Google access, while Canada and Australia have insisted on blurring out faces and license plates as a condition of entry.

This was yet another prompt for Google to reconsider its claim on public photographs. As a means of assuaging growing privacy concerns, they developed an application that would automatically blur faces and license plates beyond recognition. The response to this new feature was positive, but it did not succeed in staving off all lawsuits, as they didn't consider the privacy breach in photographing property. In April 2008, a Pittsburg couple sued Google for invasion of privacy and trespassing, asserting that the Street View feature reduced the value of their home. Aaron and

Christine Boring (*Boring vs. Google*, 2009) claimed that the "major component of their purchase decision was a desire for privacy" and Google's photographs compromised the integrity of that privacy. They also claimed that because they live on a private road, simply driving down the street with car-mounted cameras was an act of trespassing. This case is interesting because it is the first instance of a privacy suit against Google that was focused on property. To what extent should one's personal property be protected from being added to Google's "official record" of the searchable world?

The town of North Oaks, Minnesota has positioned itself at the forefront of this battle. The city has banned Google from taking Street View photographs, claiming, in a manner similar to the Borings, that because all of its town roads are private, Google has no authority to photograph them. This St Paul suburb of about 4,500 people was the first city to take action against Google's efforts, arguing that photographs taken from private streets are an act of trespassing, while satellite photographs are not (Amouth, 2008). They sent a letter in January 2008 asking that all photographs be taken down and destroyed. Google complied. Legal questions aside, the case of North Oaks points to some limits in the social tolerance for being mapped. This discomfort, while some of it surely opportunistic, is reflective of a perceived loss of agency and control over private spaces. In other words, what was previously perceived as private (private streets, somebody's image, one's house) is made public by Google. On a macro level, it is not difficult to comprehend the benefits of making close-up images of the world searchable; but on a micro level, it is necessary to contend with the fact that the world is comprised of people and their data. Making the world searchable is equated to locating and identifying users. Making everything findable presupposes that everyone wants to be found.

But Google's philosophy has always been that it is better to apologize than ask for permission.[1] The privacy complaints about Street View were surely anticipated – tiny details in the larger vision of making the world searchable. For Google, the attitude of not wanting to be found is a relic. They have been successful in selling that culture shift. These concerns are fringe; for most of us, being found (both by oneself and others) is tantamount to socialization. Getting on the map is a virtue, a marker of participation in a culture that, through no small effort from Google, values location.

The example of Google Maps points to a broader phenomenon. The possibility of having one's location information disclosed prompts serious concerns about the invasion of one's privacy and fears of surveillance, especially when the person being located has no apparent control over who accesses that location information. These issues are most evident when it comes to location-based services (LBS) (many of which we discussed in Chapter 2). LBS provide location-specific information for anyone with a GPS-equipped mobile phone. This information can come in the form of advertisements, coupons, restaurant reviews, Wikipedia articles or information about the location of nearby services, such as gas stations or coffee shops. While these services do not necessarily reveal their users' locations to nearby people, users must allow the service provider to pinpoint their location to receive the desired local information. And this information is often unknowingly shared with commercial partners, such as corporate sponsors, and application developers. As a subset of LBS, location-based social networks (LBSNs) not only transmit the users' location information to the service provider, but also share these locations with members of the users' social networks. For example, a Loopt user might be able to share their location with known buddies in their "friends" list, or – if they are using LooptMix – with anybody in the vicinity who is using Loopt.

The disclosure of one's location either to service providers or to peers is often framed as an invasion of privacy – in this case, locational privacy. There are two main fears related to losing locational privacy: the fear of top-down surveillance (mostly from the government and advertising companies), and the fear of collateral surveillance, that is, disclosing one's location to other people (de Souza e Silva & Frith, 2010b). One of the core privacy concerns when using any type of LBS is whether location information will be provided to the government. Another common concern is that service providers will share this information with advertisers.

Almost all LBS business models are based on location-based advertising. LBSNs, such as Loopt, Foursquare, Whrrl, and Google Latitude are all provided to the user for free. The easiest way to monetize these services is through advertising. For example, when checking into a location in Foursquare, users can find coupons for nearby retail shops, which typically include extra benefits for the mayor of that location. Foursquare motivates participation through its internal structure of competition (badges and mayorships), as well as through its external reward structure (coupons and free stuff). Advertisements actually become a reward for the user. Location makes advertising relevant to the user, almost like impulse purchasing in a supermarket checkout line. The assortment of candy bars and mints displayed in checkout lines is there to satisfy the immediate desires of shoppers in an impromptu fashion. Likewise, location-based advertising is based on a just-in-time model of consumer needs. One typically does not go to Foursquare to find coupons. But when coupons appear and are relevant both to past consumer behavior and the location of the consumer, they motivate impulse purchases.[2]

But it is often not clear to consumers what LBS developers do with the users' location information. If location information is provided to advertisers, as the example above demonstrates, consumers most often have no choice but to receive ads. They also generally cannot choose the type of advertisement they receive, and have no clue about which companies receive updates about their location. At this point, the privacy policies of LBSNs are not clear to most consumers. The Federal Communications Commission (FCC) requires that services obtain consent from users before targeting them with mobile advertising, but that consent is often buried in the fine print of user agreements. Many users, however, are willing to put up with these privacy statements if they see value in the type of information they are receiving.

As has Raynes-Goldie (2010) has noted, "By 2003, the number of privacy pragmatists – that is, people who are concerned about their privacy but are willing to trade some of it for something beneficial – had risen" when compared both to privacy fundamentalists and to people unconcerned about privacy. Similarly, Luann Lasalle in the *Globe and Mail* affirmed, "These [LBS] are great services if you're knowledgeable of the tradeoff, if you understand what you're giving up to get the service" (Lasalle, 2009). This is in line with previous research, which states that users are willing to give out private information depending on their perception of the usefulness of the application offered to them.[3] So, as LBS become popular, users might be more willing to disclose location information depending on the type of service received. Indeed, according to ABI Research (2009), "the number of subscribers to handset-based LBS doubled in 2008 to more than 18 million." The same report attests that while navigation continues to lead in terms of total subscribers, location-based social networking has among the highest year-to-year growth rates of mobile services. This would suggest that simply disclosing one's location is not a problem for the average user. Disclosing location information only really becomes a problem when users are unaware of who owns the information about their location, and with whom their location is being shared.

Between February and June 2009, Adriana de Souza e Silva and Jordan Frith (2010b) analyzed major world and US print and web publications (e.g. *The Globe and Mail, The New York Times, The Guardian, eWeek.com, CNN.com, Business Week Online*) to get insights about how popular press outlets were referring to location-based media. Based on their study, the most common privacy concern was that government was using location data to surveil people. For example, an *eWeek* article by Roy Mark from March 2009 put it this way: "When it comes to government surveillance, the legal interface between law enforcement and your phone and Internet service providers is a shadowy place, and it's often unclear what kinds of data companies are willing to provide to the government" (Mark, 2009). Unknowingly sharing location information with the government is frequently associated with a form of top-down surveillance, which is usually described in sensationalist language such as: "A truly Orwellian development that has been described by privacy campaigners as 'a catastrophic corruption of consent'" (Warren, 2009 in the *Guardian*).

So, even if one does know who potentially accesses location information (in this case, the government), not knowing what the government can do with this information is a major concern. Within this context, locational privacy deserves the same type of treatment as other legal issues. According to Mark's article in *eWeek*: "It's clear that your location information is the content of a private communication between you and your friends, and that it deserves the same legal protections against wiretapping as the content of your phone calls or your e-mails" (Mark, 2009).

The concern about the government (or in some cases large corporations) tracking your every move is often accompanied by another form of perceived privacy breach. Collateral surveillance or "people tracking" (*CBC News*, 2009) is the act of letting others – generally, those you know – know where you are. LBSNs and games are often the target of such concerns. These practices are associated with a loss of control over one's personal space. For example, a *Newsday* article by Emi Endo had this to say: "Thanks to the sweet/creepy new Google Latitude, [stalking is] easier than ever" (Endo, 2009). The "fear of being tracked," as the awareness of location is generally described (Mason, 2009 in the *Daily Telegraph*), is frequently connected to unknowingly giving up location information. For instance, the *New York Times* warned that "you may use your phone to find friends and restaurants, but somebody else may be using your phone to find you and find out about you" (Markoff, 2009). In this case, "somebody else" is generally someone we know, as the article by David Rowan (2009) in the *Times* warns us: "Let's just imagine that a jealous partner gains access to your unattended phone and enables Latitude without your knowledge." News outlets addressing these fears point to situations where people have lost control over their location information.

However, they have not ceded control to large entities; rather, they have ceded control only to their social network. When other people can take control over one's location information, they take away one's control over their private space.

As a result of the popular discourse around LBS, software designers have created safeguards for users to control their privacy settings, such as the ability to select which friends are allowed in their network, or the ability to hide location from specific users (de Souza e Silva & Frith, 2010a). Currently most location-based applications are designed with three main functions in order to allow users to control privacy settings (Arran, 2009): first, the opt-in function that requires users to download the application to their mobile phones and explicitly accept the software request to use the user's location; second, the adjustable accuracy function, allowing users to adjust how precise their location will be displayed to friends – or the option to update their location manually (in which case they can lie about their real location); and third, the out-of-reach function: the ability to block location awareness if the mobile phone is lost or stolen.

However, users' comfort in the security of their information, or their ability to prevent location information from being accessed by unknown users, is still quite volatile. This volatility is likely caused by the lack of clarity in the privacy settings within many of these applications. It is often difficult to understand what the settings mean, or even if they can be adjusted. For example, the Foursquare default setting is to share location information with all members of a user's network. The user can manually turn that feature off every time she checks into a location, but there is no way to choose some members of a network over others. Additionally, when checking into a place with Foursquare, users can automatically see other Foursquare users in the vicinity, even if they were not added to their network.

As de Souza e Silva and Frith (2010b) discovered, disclosing information about location in LBSNs is often characterized as scary, creepy, connected to unwanted surveillance, and an invasion of privacy, especially when users have no control of who can access it. Similar fears have been reported in the context of location-based mobile games (LBMGs). In their study of the game Mogi, Licoppe and Inada (2009) describe a case perceived as stalking by one female player who could see a nearby, unidentified player on her mobile screen. Despite repeated requests by the female player, the anonymous player never disclosed his identity, resulting in feelings of fear that the digital stalking would cross over into physical space. This example demonstrates that awareness of location might lead to power asymmetries. Similarly, Licoppe and Inada (2006) describe situations in which both players see each other on their mobile screen, but only one claims he can see the other in the physical space of the city, leading to uncomfortable and almost fearful feelings from the player under the risk of losing his anonymity. They also note that at the core of an LBMG experience – which they describe as a culture of proximity – is the assumption that one's location is public, so such behaviors (which treat location as private) actually run counter to user expectations of net localities. However, embedded in the very assumptions and fears of Mogi players is a shift in the nature of how individuals perceive and acknowledge each other in city spaces. With the popularization of location-aware technologies, people's locations become public and available to all. Licoppe and Inada suggest that the wide use of location-based applications will force us to question how we manage social interactions in public spaces, leading to "the development of an interaction order founded on the public character of locations" (p. 123). But if location information is public, then how can one maintain any claims of privacy as it pertains to location? Perhaps net localities, by pushing the boundaries of what is private and what is public, force us to reconsider how we understand privacy and surveillance in contemporary society.

Rethinking privacy and surveillance

While an in depth discussion of privacy and surveillance is outside the scope of this book, understanding how these terms change over time might help us to analyze how and why location-aware technologies challenge how we understand privacy and surveillance, and consequently public and private spaces.

In his book *Understanding Privacy*, the legal scholar Daniel Solove (2008) describes the various conceptions of privacy throughout the nineteenth and twentieth centuries. Solove criticizes these conceptions as being either too narrow or too broad, and proposes that we should instead understand privacy according to specific contextual situations. Conceptions of privacy have changed over the years; and at any given time, there is considerable disagreement about its meaning. In American society, privacy was originally imagined as "the right to be let alone," following Samuel Warren and Louis Brandeis famous article "The Right to Privacy" (Warren & Brandeis, 1890). However, the idea of privacy has also been frequently addressed in relation to forms of power: as power to limit access to the self, power to conceal information about oneself, and power to have control over one's personal information. The majority of privacy issues that arise within net localities are related to the fear of losing control and power over one's (locational) information, which has traditionally been considered private.

As privacy is related to power, so is surveillance. George Orwell's novel *1984* (2002 [1949]) is often evoked in discussions of power and surveillance. In his novel, an all-powerful individual (Big Brother) intrusively observes other citizens through inconspicuous surveillance technologies. People live in perpetual fear of the all seeing eye of Big Brother. But the metaphors of top-down surveillance are no longer useful for understanding issues of privacy and surveillance in the context of digital databases (Solove, 2004). The traditional ways of understanding privacy (as the right to be let alone or having control over personal information) and surveillance (as a top-down form of power) need to be reconsidered in the context of net locality.

Solove (2004) suggests that while these metaphors were useful for addressing a number of privacy problems, they have severe limitations when it comes to the database problem. "The most significant shortcoming of the Big Brother metaphor is that it fails to focus on the appropriate form of power" (Solove, 2004, p. 34). Within the database logic explored by Solove, personal information is collected by machines, instead of by one individual who can watch another's every movement. The personal information collected is generally not something that one would consider "private" (e.g., name, race, marital status) and is therefore not seen as threatening. The main problem emerges, however, when this information is aggregated and used to construct what he calls "digital identities," and used by corporations to predict behavioral and consumption patterns. Users generally have no control over what is done with their personal information once it is collected.

When it comes to location information, the situation is similar. LBS privacy statements are generally vague enough that they do not inform users about what kind of information is collected, who the partners are, and what they might do with the information. So the problem is less of a Big Brother-style top-down surveillance, and more of a lack of control about the destiny of collected information. According to Solove, a more adequate metaphor to address information collection in the digital age is Franz Kafka's *The Trial*. Rather than focusing on centralized surveillance, as is the case of Big Brother, *The Trial* is about a bureaucratic system, which never informs the victim about the purpose of his trial, or the reason for information collection. The anxiety is about lack of control, and not about surveillance. In Solove's words, "the problem with databases and the practices associated with them is that they disempower people" (Solove, 2004, p. 41).[4]

Thinking of a decentralized form of power is also useful for understanding privacy and surveillance in net localities. Moving away from traditional ideas of top-down surveillance allows us to reconsider locational privacy. It is how we use information that matters, not just our ability to keep it secret. So, simply disclosing one's location is not a problem *per se*, but it becomes one when users have no control over who accesses it and what is done with it. Often, when location information is aggregated through applications such as Citysense, it is used to predict people's behavior in the city. While this practice is not overtly harmful to the individual, it can be used to deliver location-specific advertisements or to create profiles of particular areas of the city that could result in exclusionary practices.

Indeed, what we are witnessing with the development of net locality is a shift in the traditional model of surveillance toward a model of decentralized and all-encompassing surveillance in which all individuals in the network know the position of all others. The actual function of this surveillance is unclear for most end users, and the threat unspecified, which is exactly what makes people fear the disclosure of their location.[5]

So, while location-aware applications typically present a very clear use of location information, they prompt anxiety because of the absoluteness in which they locate the user. Someone or something knows exactly where you are at any given time. Perhaps these privacy concerns will continue to grow. But more likely the terms of the privacy debate will so radically depart from its present framework that what constitutes a breach and what satisfies consumer demands is now impossible to predict. Not only do location-aware technologies put privacy into question by making location public, but they also reorient public spaces by allowing users to privatize them.

The Privatization of Public Spaces

The popular press is fond of warning us about our impending "loss of privacy" with the use of location-aware technologies – but what the media rarely acknowledge, however, is that the distinction between private and public is socially constructed, and therefore variable and constantly changing. The separation of public and private can be traced back at least as far as the Ancient Greeks. In Greek society, the public was the place for politics, such as the *Agora*, where things "could be seen and heard by everybody" (Arendt, 1958, p. 50). The private, on the other hand, was the place of property, and the family. Private spaces were then secluded closed spaces, separate from the public open spaces. But according to Arendt, the divide between the public and the private is no longer so pronounced. When eighteenth century economies expanded, things that were previously private, such as the necessities of "life, labor, and reproduction," took over the public realm, transforming it into a "sphere for the satisfaction of our material needs" (D'Entrèves, 1994, p. 58). In modernity, Arendt argues that the public and the private have been subsumed under the *social*. Throughout history, we see a constant shift and renegotiation of the social boundaries between private and public.

Because technology also constitutes society and is shaped and influenced by it (Castells, 2000), the development of transportation and communication technologies have contributed to the constant shifting of boundaries between the public and the private. For example, Gant and Kiesler (2002) note that with the popularization of rail transport in the mid-nineteenth century, the separation between work (public) and personal life (private) grew more definitive as people started commuting. While transportation technologies contributed to the creation of more distinct boundaries between the public and the private, communication technologies such as the telephone, the telegraph, and the television brought the public within the private space of the home (Boltanski, 1999; Moores, 2004).

Every time the socially established boundaries between the public and the private have been challenged, technologies have been perceived as a threat either to personal privacy or to public spaces. For example, critics have accused portable mobile media, like the Walkman and the iPod, of tainting public spaces with the private. Mobile listening devices raised concerns about the maintenance of public space, as Hosokawa (1984, 1987) and Chalmers (1994) show, and we can see the same phenomenon with the iPod each time someone listens to music on a pair of headphones far too loudly on a public bus. More recently, scholars and critics have looked at how mobile and networked technologies have served to blur these boundaries.[6] They force us to re-think how we understand public spaces as spaces that include networked interactions.

Mobile phone use in public spaces can still be annoying and distracting. But, as we described in Chapter 4, people are changing their practices or their responses to others to better accommodate this new reality. People are both more likely to stop what they are doing to engage in a phone conversation; and at the same time, they are more accustomed to those who don't. And of course, the use of location-aware technologies is undergoing a similar period of transition and acceptance. Most pronounced is the way in which these technologies are contributing to a renegotiation of the boundaries between public and private.

This is most clear in regard to the control over personal space. Traditionally, the private space of the home has represented a controlled personal space in clear distinction from "uncontrolled" public spaces. But, net localities challenge this. Users can wield more control over these public spaces by uploading and accessing place-specific information. As Eric Gordon (2009) has noted, in a net locality, "private space is no longer defined solely as control over a geographic domain; it is control over the access and production of data within flexible information flows" (p. 26). So, beyond the traditional challenge of the public encroaching upon the private (transforming personal location information into public data), net localities exacerbate the problem of the private encroaching upon the public (a user's ability to aggregate location data in accordance with their immediate and specific needs).

Implications for control and exclusion

When users are not confident in their control over their privacy settings, they fear the loss of privacy. However, when users feel in control of their personal information and their ability to use it, they celebrate the expansion of traditional definitions of privacy. Indeed, giving up location information might be acceptable, as long as users are in control of it and aware of what it entails. The Google Latitude privacy settings allow users to lie about their location by inserting it manually. Having one's position visualized on a map at a fake location theoretically gives users the ultimate control over their surroundings. So, although traditional notions of privacy – the "right to be let alone" – are still factors in how people perceive these services, the ability to control one's personal space often outweighs traditional privacy concerns.

If public spaces have conventionally been perceived as "open," uncontrolled spaces, then private spaces are "secluded," controlled spaces. In other words, it is the ability to exert control over spaces that transforms them into perceived private spheres. People once considered the telephone, the TV, and the radio technologies that brought the public into the private, with the telephone being the worst offender (Marvin, 1990). Conversely, people thought that mobile technologies, such as the book, the Walkman and the iPod brought the private into the public. They were not just means of escaping public space – they were means of controlling it.[7]

All the above-mentioned mobile technologies, however, frame users' interactions with public spaces by introducing external references. For example, a book's narrative is not necessarily about the place where it is being read; the voice of a mobile phone conversation generally comes from elsewhere; and the iPod's songs are loaded independent of location. Conversely, location-aware technologies draw information from the physical surroundings. For example, a user equipped with a GPS-enabled mobile phone in Times Square who opens the application WikiMe is able to read Wikipedia articles about Times Square. Similarly, if she decides to write a Twitter post about Times Square, that piece of information will be coded with the longitude and latitude (longlat) coordinates of that place. Location-based advertisements are delivered to users based on their location in physical space. Besides accessing place-specific information in the form of articles, nearby restaurant reviews, coupons, and the location of surrounding gas stations and cafeterias, LBSNs help users find other people.

One of the unfortunate and obvious side effects of the use of these applications is the potential for a different type of social divide between those who have access to the technology and those who do not. It is no longer simply location that is a determinant or marker of class, but also location awareness. The use of location-aware technologies can exclude those who do not use them. For example, if someone is riding on a bus and opens Foursquare, he'll be able to play and interact with other passengers who have Foursquare on their phones. He might also come to personally know these people, since they have some things in common (both like games, own a smart phone, and are riding the same bus). But the mobile interface might make him simultaneously pay attention to other nearby Foursquare players and ignore those passengers who do not own the application. This is distinct from the early days of mobile phones, when the devices were blamed for disconnecting people from their surroundings. Location-aware technologies generally do the exact opposite – they draw people's attention to their surrounding space. The danger here, however, is that they could introduce inequalities into that space. So although these technologies increase the potential for communication and coordination with people who possess them, they might reduce communication with those who do not.

Spaces can become "overfiltered." Users can opt to encounter the same people and things, just as they tend to do on the web (Sunstein, 2006). In her empirical study of the mobile social network Dodgeball, communication scholar Lee Humphreys (2007) observed that its users did not necessarily meet more people, but instead hung out at different places with the same people. Humphreys also found that people used Dodgeball to meet existing friends out on the town, and in meeting those friends, did not necessarily connect to the general public, "thus leading to a kind of social molecularization" (p. 356). She affirmed that even when users did "meet new people through Dodgeball, these people were fairly demographically similar" (p. 356). In other words, the diversity of urban spaces may become masked in net localities. Rather than chance encounters of difference, she suggests that mobile social networks facilitate chance encounters of sameness.

But this analysis discounts the nuance of net localities and the importance of urban spaces for constructing social meaning. The urge to be among familiar things, people and spaces, however, is not solely a consequence of the use of new digital technologies, nor is it new. As we discussed in Chapter 5, the blasé attitude in the nineteenth century was a cultivated appearance of indifference used to protect the city dweller from the constant flood of stimulation. People in cities have always had the capacity to filter out what they did not want to see – from adopting an attitude to wearing earphones to consulting mobile devices. In the case of net localities, it is difficult to conclude that simply because there are filters that users will always employ them to encounter self-similar events. In fact, it may be that just the opposite is true. Instead of redirecting users' attention to like-minded and physically absent networks, location-aware technologies direct the user to their immediate surroundings, which will always encompass some difference. The user can be near a diversity of things and people because the search filter is that which is physically near.

And this starts with the pursuit of familiarity. If a user knows there are people like her in a certain place, she might be more comfortable going there. So, a place that is unfamiliar might gain familiarity if people using location-aware applications can "see" their friends before going there (Sutko & de Souza e Silva, in press). Take Citysense as an example. The mobile application displays heatmaps that illustrate spatial concentrations of people in a given space. If a user notices that a number of people are congregating at a little known public beach, which she is particularly fond of, she might be compelled to go there. This follows the traditional public space model, as presented by Whyte (1980), in which the presence of co-located people validates a place. For example, he considered the Seagram Building plaza in Manhattan a "good public space" because of the likelihood of interpersonal encounters. The people one encounters in familiar places are themselves somewhat familiar because of their presence and affinity for the shared place. The difference, however, is that in the case of Citysense, the assessment of a place is done remotely via a mobile phone screen.

But this changes the nature of communication. There is some evidence that the proximity of people in net localities creates new kinds of tensions amongst users. For example, Nicolas Nova and Fabien Girardin (2009) tested their LBMG CatchBob! (Nova & Girardin, 2007) in two modes: with and without mutual location awareness. One of their findings was that the presence of location awareness, that is, automatic detection of players' locations, led to a decrease in communication within the group. While this finding seems obvious (if you have information about each other's location, you do not need to call and ask for it), it points to changes in how people communicate in net localities. Some verbal communication is replaced by digital inference. Regardless of how people correspond, it is clear that location-aware technologies facilitate a diversity of experiences for those who possess them by allowing users to infer qualities about strangers based on where they are, and likewise, infer qualities about strange locations based on people they know.

This, however, does not preclude the fact that people who do not have access to location-aware technologies might experience net localities differently and be less likely to interact with other people. David Wood and Stephen Graham (2005) call this "differential mobility." They distinguish between two types of mobility: high mobility, pertaining to those few with easy access, and slow mobility, which includes the majority with difficult, blocked access. In this sense, mobility is directly related to power. At their core, location-aware technologies are mobile technologies and will likely contribute to this differential mobility. For example, the version of Loopt on the Google Android phones provides place-specific traffic updates (Loopt, 2008). Location-aware technologies allow only individuals with access to enhance their mobility. However, as Wood and Graham note, differential mobility has always existed. From the moment some people rode or were carried while others walked, there have existed differences in mobility which reflect and reinforce social structures (2005, p. 177). But distinct from previous forms of mobile technologies, location-aware devices do more than contribute to differential mobility; they lead to differential spaces.

LBSNs change the perception of urban spaces for the "in" crowd. Those who do not have access to these technologies will not be able to communicate with the social network. The consequences of this exclusion may affect more than the communication between people; it may affect our perception and understanding of public spaces (de Souza e Silva & Frith, 2010a, p. 498). Individuals equipped with these technologies have the opportunity to interact with a space that is markedly different from the space perceived by individuals who do not have access to the technology. For example, two individuals walk side-by-side down a crowded street – one perceives the street as only a physical space and the other perceives it as a net locality. The physical space is unchanged for the individual excluded from the LBSN while the member of the social network perceives the physical space embedded with digital information.

Previously, individuals could listen to music, read, or daydream to "go away" as Goffman called it. But the space they occupied was still the same space occupied by other people sharing that physical location. Location-aware technologies change this. Users can "customize" public spaces with features like LooptMix, which allow a user to choose what type of person shows up on her map. This customization of space, whether through applications like WikiMe or Loopt, has the potential to detract from the shared experience of urban spaces. It might thus be argued that these applications create a type of "differential public space," in which physically co-located people experience things very differently. How will the creation of a "differential space" affect the relationships between people using location-aware technologies and those not connected to the network? How will each set of people experience "public" spaces differently? Although the answers to these questions are not clear at this point, these issues will certainly shape how we interact with net localities in the future.

Power in Net Localities

According to Manuel Castells (2009), "The sources of social power in our world have not changed fundamentally from our historical experience" (p. 50). What has changed, however, is the context in which power relationships operate. This has changed in two major ways: "it is primarily constructed around the articulation between the global and the local, and it is primarily organized around networks" (p. 50). These changes are each reflected in net localities. The global and the local are blurring in physical spaces through the perpetual, if unequal, access to digital networks. While net localities provide an unprecedented control to some, through exclusion, they threaten to further exacerbate existing inequities. This all hinges on our changing perceptions of privacy. While the distinction between public and private has shifted with each new communication and transportation technology, net locality marks a more significant shift. Issues of privacy and control are intimately connected to users' locations and their awareness of local spaces. Paul Dourish (2006) asserts that mobile technologies do not create an urban utopia. The image of users wandering the city with unlimited information at their fingertips "fail(s) to acknowledge . . . the systems of power and control within which those tactics emerge (and against which they should be read)" (p. 5).

Governments can use location awareness to track how fast people are driving; some products are being marketed for individuals to track their spouses or their children; advertisers can easily use location information to target people with relevant ads. But net localities are also spaces of consumption. Simply because net localities are infused with commercial and surveillance applications does not mean that the interactions innovated there are shallow or antithetical to meaningful, non-market-based social exchanges. Urban interactions have never been without commercial influence. From signs to billboards to newspapers, the urban environment has always been populated by information and messaging that has influenced the behavior of people. Net localities indicate yet another change in a constantly evolving urban environment of commercialism and social exchange. The divisions between public and private, inclusive and exclusive, have to be reconsidered in light of these technologies and practices.

Notes

1 This was certainly true with their books initiative, their effort to copy the entire contents of five major research libraries, including Harvard, New York Public, and University of Michigan. While this effort has resulted in lawsuits from book publishers, before the complaints even surfaced, the project was well on its way to completion.

2 This is similar to the Google advertising strategy on the web that directs ads to users based on search histories, email content, and consumer behavior, and makes relevant commodities only clicks away from a given web "site."

3 For examples of this research, see Barkuus & Dey, 2003; Ackerman, Cranor, & Reagle, 1999; Ackerman, Kempf, & Miki, 2003.

4 Manuel Castells (2009) also refutes the idea of a centralized power in the network society. He argues that "it is precisely because there is no unified power elite capable of keeping the programming and switching operations of all important networks under its control that more subtle, complex, and negotiated systems of power enforcement must be established" (p. 47).

5 Since the popularization of camera phones and portable camcorders, it is clear that we have moved away from the Orwellian model of top-down surveillance and Michel Foucault's idea of the panopticon (Foucault, 1995). Indeed, Gilles Deleuze (1992) already emphasized the shift from disciplinary societies, represented by confined spaces (prison, school, hospital) and a one-to-many model of control, to the societies of control, represented by open spaces (corporations and stock markets) in which the control model is not as evident but is nonetheless continuous and unlimited. More recently, Steve Mann (Mann, Noland, & Wellman, 2003) proposed the concept of *sousveillance* to describe ways by which individuals might be empowered through the use of portable communication technologies such as mobile phones and camcorders (de Souza e Silva & Sutko, 2008). Mann's idea of *sousveillance* emphasizes a bottom-up approach by which users are able to neutralize surveillance by inverting its mechanism (i.e., allowing individuals to observe and control corporations and the government). However, as Matt Adams from Blast Theory points out, "we

are still locked in an Orwellian paradigm that has long since passed its sell by date" (de Souza e Silva & Sutko, 2009, p. 81). And he adds that *sousveillance* is also nothing new, given that it has been with us since the rise of the camcorder. Although it is possible to claim that today individuals own an increasing number of *sousveillance* tools, what these tools generally contribute to is not a neutralization of surveillance per se, but rather a creation of other forms of collateral, decentralized and open surveillance by which everybody is able to keep track of everybody.

6 Some notable criticisms on the blurring of public and private include Gant & Kiesler, 2002; Ling, 2004; Katz & Aakhus, 2002; Puro, 2002; Fortunati, 2002.
7 For more discussion about personal spaces in public settings, see Manguel, 1997; Bull, 2001, 2006; Sterne, 2003.

References

ABI, Research. (2009). Mobile location based services: Applications, platforms, positioning technology, handset evolution, and business model migration. Retrieved November 1, 2010 from http://www.abiresearch.com/research/ 1003335-Mobile + Location + Based + Services

Ackerman, M. S., Cranor, L., & Reagle, J. (1999). Privacy in e-commerce: Examining user scenarios and privacy preferences. *Proceedings of the 1st ACM Conference in Electronic Commerce*, 1–8. DOI: 10.1145/336992.336995

Ackerman, L., Kempf, J., & Miki, T. (2003). *Wireless location privacy: A report on law and policy in the United States, the European Union, and Japan*. San Jose, CA: DoCoMo. Retrieved November 1, 2010 from http://www.docomolabs -usa.com/pdf/DCL-TR2003-001.pdf

Amouth, D. (2008, June 2). Small Minnesota town tells Google to take a hike. *PCWorld*. Retrieved November 1, 2010 from http://blogs.pcworld.com/ staffblog/archives/007044.html

Andrejevic, M. (2007). Surveillance in the digital enclosure. *Communication Review*, 10, 295–317.

Arendt, H. (1958). *The human condition*. Chicago, IL: University of Chicago Press.

Arran, T. (2009). Locating privacy. *GPS Business News*. Retrieved November 1, 2010 from http://www.gpsbusinessnews.com/Locating-Privacy_a1474.html

Barkuus, L., & Dey, A. (2003). Location-based services for mobile telephony: A study of users' privacy concerns. *Proceedings of the INTERACT 2003, 9TH IFIP TC13 International Conference on Human-Computer Interaction*, July. Retrieved November 1, 2010 from http://intel-research.net/Publications/ Berkeley/072920031046_154.pdf

Boltanski, L. (1999). *Distant suffering: Morality, media and politics*. New York: Cambridge University Press.

Boring, A. C., & Boring, C. vs. Google, Inc., 2:08-cv-00694-ARH (Western District of Pennsylvania, 2009).

Bull, M. (2001). The world according to sound: Investigating the world of walkman users. *New Media and Society, 3*, 179–197.

Bull, M. (2006). Investigating the culture of mobile listening: From Walkman to iPod. In O'Hara, K., & Brown, B. (Eds.), *Consuming music together: Social and collaborative aspects of music consumption technologies* (pp. 131–149). Amsterdam: Springer Netherlands.

Castells, M. (2000) *The rise of the network society.* Oxford: Blackwell.

Castells, M. (2009). *Communication power.* Oxford: Oxford University Press.

CBC, News. (2009, February 4). Google people tracker raises privacy issues. *CBC News*, Technology and Science section. Retrieved November 1, 2010 from http://www.cbc.ca/technology/story/2009/02/04/google-latitude.html

Chalmers, I. (1994). *Migrancy, culture, and identity.* London: Routledge.

de Souza e Silva, A., & Frith, J. (2010a). Locative mobile social networks: Mapping communication and location in urban spaces. *Mobilities, 5*(4), 485–506.

de Souza e Silva, A., & Frith, J. (2010b). Locational privacy in public spaces: Media discourses on location-aware mobile technologies. *Communication, Culture and Critique, 3*(4), 503–525. DOI: 10.1111/j.1753–9137.2010.01083.x

de Souza e Silva, A., & Sutko, D. M. (2008). Playing life and living play: How hybrid reality games reframe space, play, and the ordinary. *Critical Studies in Media Communication, 25*(5), 447–765.

de Souza e Silva, A., & Sutko, D. M. (2009). On the social and political implications of hybrid reality gaming: An interview with Matt Adams from Blast Theory (pp. 71–82). In *Digital cityscapes: Merging digital and urban playspaces.* New York: Peter Lang.

D'Entrèves, M. P. (1994). *The political philosophy of Hannah Arendt.* London: Routledge.

Deleuze, G. (1992). Postscript on the societies of control. *October 59*, Winter 1992, 3–7. Cambridge, MA: MIT Press.

Dourish, P. (2006) Re-space-ing place: "Place" and "Space" ten years on. *Proceedings of the 2006 20th Anniversary Conference on Computer Supported Cooperative Work* (pp. 299–308). Banff, Alberta, Canada.

Endo, E. (2009, February 5). Google online tool lets you track friends. *Newsday*, p. A08.

Fortunati, L. (2002). Italy: Stereotypes, true and false. In Katz, J., & Aakhus, M. (Eds.), *Perpetual contact: Mobile communication, private talk, public performance* (pp. 42–62). Cambridge: Cambridge University Press.

Foucault, M. (1995). *Discipline and punish: The birth of the prison.* 2nd Vintage Books edn. New York: Vintage Books.

Gant, D., & Kiesler, S. (2002). Blurring the boundaries: Cell phones, mobility, and the line between work and personal life. In Brown, B., Green, N., & Harper, R. (Eds.), *Wireless world: Social and interactional aspects of the mobile age* (pp. 121–131). London: Springer-Verlag.

Gordon, E. (2009). Redefining the local: The distinction between located information and local knowledge in location-based games. In de Souza e Silva, A., &

Sutko, D. M. (Eds.), *Digital cityscapes: Merging physical and digital playspaces* (pp. 21–36). New York: Peter Lang.

Hosokawa, S. (1984). The Walkman effect. *Popular Music, 4,* 165–180.

Hosokawa, S. (1987). *Der Walkman-Effekt.* Berlin: Merve.

Humphreys, L. (2007). Mobile social networks and social practice: A case study of Dodgeball. *Journal of Computer-Mediated Communication, 13*(1). Retrieved November 1, 2010 from http://jcmc.indiana.edu/vol13/issue1/humphreys .html

Kafka, F. (1998 [1925]). *The trial.* New York: Shocken Books.

Katz, J., & Aakhus, M. (2002). *Perpetual contact: Mobile communication, private talk, public performance.* Cambridge, MA: Cambridge University Press.

Laselle, L. (2009, February 29). Where Google meets Facebook meets GPS. *The Globe and Mail,* Globe Life section, p. L3. Retrieved November 1, 2010 from http://www.theglobeandmail.com/life/article10137.ece

Licoppe, C., & Inada, Y. (2006) Emergent uses of a multiplayer location-aware mobile game: The interactional consequences of mediated encounters. *Mobilities, 1*(1): 39–61.

Licoppe, C., & Inada, Y. (2009). Mediated co-proximity and its dangers in a location-aware community: A case of stalking. In de Souza e Silva, A., & Sutko, D. M. (Eds.), *Digital cityscapes: Merging digital and urban playspaces* (pp. 100–128). New York: Peter Lang.

Ling, R. (2004). *The mobile connection: The cell phone's impact on society.* San Francisco, CA: Morgan Kaufman.

Loopt., (2008). G1 users, Loopt has arrived! Retrieved November 1, 2010 from http://blog.loopt.com/page/16/

Manguel, A. (1997). *A history of reading.* New York: Penguin Books.

Mann, S., Nolan, J., & Wellman, B. (2003). Sousveillance: Inventing and wearing usable computing devices for data collection in surveillance environments. *Surveillance and Society, 1*(3), 331–355.

Mark, R. (2009, March 5). Google promises memory loss for latitude. *eWeek,* Messaging and Collaboration section. Retrieved November 1, 2010 from http://www.eweek.com/c/a/Messaging-and-Collaboration/Google-Promises -Memory-Loss-for-Latitude/

Markoff, J. (2009, February 16). The cellphone, navigating our lives. *The New York Times.* Finance section. Retrieved November 1, 2010 from http://www .nytimes.com/2009/02/17/science/17map.html

Marvin, C. (1990). *When old technologies were new.* Oxford: Oxford University Press.

Mason, R. (2009 April, 27). Acxiom: The company that knows if you own a cat or if you're right-handed. *Daily Telegraph,* Finance section, p. 5. Retrieved November 1, 2010 from http://www.telegraph.co.uk/finance/newsbysector/ retailandconsumer/5231752/Acxiom-the-company-that-knows-if-you-own -a-cat-or-if-youre-right-handed.html

Moores, S. (2004). The doubling of place: Electronic media, time-space arrange-ments, and social relationships. In Couldry, N., & McCarthy, A. (Eds.),

Media/space: Place, scale and culture in a media age (pp. 21–36). London and New York: Routledge.

Nova, N., & Girardin, F. (2007). CatchBob! [Game]. CRAFT – Swiss Federal Institute of Technology, Lausanne, Switzerland.

Nova, N., & Girardin, F. (2009). Framing issues for the design of location-based games. In de Souza e Silva, A., & Sutko, D. M. (Eds.), *Digital cityscapes: Merging digital and urban playspaces* (pp. 168–186). New York: Peter Lang.

Orwell, G. (2002 [1949]). *1984.* New York: Rosetta Books.

Poulsen, K. (2007). Want off Street View? Google wants your ID and a sworn statement. *Wired: Threat Level Blog.* Retrieved November 1, 2010 from http://blog.wired.com/27bstroke6/2007/06/want_off_street.html

Puro, J. P. (2002). Finland, a mobile culture. In Katz, J., & Aakhus, M. (Eds.), *Perpetual contact: Mobile communication, private talk, public performance* (pp. 19–29). Cambridge, MA: Cambridge University Press.

Raynes-Goldie, K. (2010). Aliases, creeping, and wall cleaning: Understanding privacy in the age of Facebook. *First Monday, 15*(1). Retrieved November 1, 2010 from http://firstmonday.org/htbin/cgiwrap/bin/ojs/index.php/fm/article/view/2775/2432

Rowan, D. (2009, March 28). Wired editor: Google has us all in its web. *The Times,* Saturday Review, Features, p. 4. Retrieved November 1, 2010 from http://technology.timesonline.co.uk/tol/news/tech_and_web/article5986190.ece

Solove, D. (2004). *The digital person: Technology and privacy in the information age.* New York and London: New York University Press.

Solove, D. (2008). *Understanding privacy.* New York: Harvard University Press.

Sterne, J. (2003). *The audible past: Cultural origins of sound reproduction.* Durham, NC: Duke University Press.

Sunstein, C. (2006). *Infotopia: How many minds produce knowledge.* Oxford: Oxford University Press.

Sutko, D. M., & de Souza e Silva, A. (in press). Location aware mobile media and urban sociability. *New Media & Society.*

Warren, P. (2009, April 2). The end of privacy? Forget Street View, there is a far more subtle – and pervasive – invasion of your private life being carried out – this time through your mobile phone. *The Guardian,* Technology section, p. 1. Retrieved November 1, 2010 from http://www.guardian.co.uk/technology/2009/apr/02/google-privacy-mobile-phone-industry

Warren, S., & Brandeis, L. (1890). The right to privacy. *Harvard Law Review,* 4(5). Retrieved November 1, 2010 from http://groups.csail.mit.edu/mac/classes/6.805/articles/privacy/Privacy_brand_warr2.html

Whyte, W. H. (1980). *The social life of small urban spaces.* New York: Project for Public Places.

Wood, D., & Graham, S. (2005). Permeable boundaries in the software-sorted society: Surveillance and the differentiation of mobility. In Sheller, M., & Urry, J. (Eds.), *Mobile technologies of the city* (pp. 177–191). London: Routledge

7

Globalization

Net localities are spaces embedded with networked connections. So far in this book we have addressed the social practices that contribute to the development of net localities – including mapping, mobile annotations, location-based games and social networks, and the implications of these practices for urban spaces, community interaction, and perceptions of privacy and surveillance. Although we described net locality primarily through examples from the United States and the United Kingdom, it is indeed a global phenomenon.[1]

The web is often praised as one of the main drivers of globalization. The ability to instantaneously connect remote places, the logic goes, can render physical distances irrelevant and make the world seem smaller. This concept of globalization emphasizes how the global influences the local, possibly endangering local cultures and practices. In Manuel Castells's terminology, globalization privileges the "space of flows" over the "space of places" (Castells, 2000). So, the value and meaning of localities in a global society come from their ability to belong to and exchange information with a global information network, rather than from their local characteristics. It thus seems that regions and localities become integrated in a global network that privileges information flows rather than places and local connections. And exactly because the web enabled information to flow more easily from place to place, predictions about the end of local cultures and the emergence of a more homogenized world have been prevalent since the 1990s (Couclelis, 2007; Canclini, 2001).

But after almost two decades since the creation of the web, it is obvious that localities never lost their importance, and that the increasing ability to

Net Locality: Why Location Matters in a Networked World, First Edition. Eric Gordon and Adriana de Souza e Silva. © 2011 Eric Gordon and Adriana de Souza e Silva. Published 2011 by Blackwell Publishing Ltd.

connect places has in fact contributed to a greater recognition of local cultures. Joshua Meyrowitz (2005) once suggested that electronic media such as TV, radio, and the web foster in their audiences a great emotional attachment to locations. For Meyrowitz, this greater connection to location occurred because these technologies allowed people to be aware of what was happening *outside* their local spaces. For example, when somebody watches news on television about a war taking place on the other side of the world, those events might change how individuals see their local surroundings. Being aware of the global enabled people to compare their local spaces to the global elsewhere, which for Meyrowitz led to a more conscious identification to local places and "more explicit passion for localities" (Meyrowitz, 2005, p. 26).

What we witness with net locality though, is different. Net locality inverts the traditional idea of globalization by focusing on how the local influences the global. Localities are not relevant because they are connected to a global network; they are relevant because they have the power to change global practices. Meyrowitz argued that we value the local because we were aware of the global. Within net locality, we value the local not only because of outside connections, but because we are constantly in touch with local knowledge and information.

Globalization has facilitated the spread of digital technologies even to the most remote parts of the world. The technologies used to interface with net localities do not change much from place to place, but their local uses are distinct. People adapt technologies to meet local needs. This is called technological appropriation, or the process through which technology users go beyond mere adoption to make the technology their own and to embed it within their local, social, cultural, economic and political practices (Bar, Pisani, & Weber, 2007). Users of technologies may modify the device, download or program new applications, and invent new unintended uses for the technology to better adapt the tool to their needs and desires. For example, the practice of "beeping" from prepaid mobile phones in developing countries entails calling another party and hanging up. After the phone rings once or twice, the other party knows to return the call or act upon some predefined message (Donner, 2005; de Souza e Silva *et al.*, in press). This is a use of technology that is responsive to the economic realities of its users. To some extent, all uses of technology by people outside of the intended market are appropriations. As Manuel Castells (2000) argues, technology is a product of social forces, shaped by the context of the society in which it is embedded.

Consider the Ilkone, which was introduced in the Middle East and Southeast Asia in 2004. The 3G mobile phone enables daily Islamic spiritual practices as it generates five automated reminders a day at prayer time and points Muslims in the direction of Mecca from 5,000 cities around the world. The phone also contains a copy of the Islamic holy book, the Koran, in both Arabic and English (*MSNBC*, 2005). Although the Ilkone has a similar technical infrastructure as other mobile phones – GPS technology, digital flash card, calendar software – its unique functionality is produced in response to the global and local practices of Islam.

Examples like this are widespread throughout the world. How networked technologies are appropriated to the meet the specific needs of people in a locality is the subject of this chapter. We have talked extensively about how net localities are manifested in the United States and the United Kingdom. We now turn our attention to how net localities are unfolding in other national contexts. Net locality is a global phenomenon that has unique resonances in different parts of the world.[2] To demonstrate this, we focus on specific examples primarily from two countries in East Asia: China and Japan. China is the fastest growing market of mobile and Internet technologies in the world; and Japan is known as the place where the first mobile phone service was launched, and where the most innovative information technologies are invented. Looking at these examples, we will explore how net localities are products of the cultures from which they emerge and how local cultures are being shaped by net localities.

Japan

A small country with a dense, digitally sophisticated population, Japan has been a leader in broadband and cellular innovations. Nippon Telephone and Telegraph (today known as NTT DOCOMO) began field tests of cellular systems as early as 1975, and Japan launched what is considered today the world's first cellular radio service in December 1979 (Goggin, 2006; Farley, 2005). Since then, Japan has led the way in 2G and 3G networks. More than any other country, the Japanese appropriation of web technologies has been focused on the mobile phone. For example, Japanese *keitai denwa* (mobile phone) users rely heavily on their mobile phones for sending and receiving email. Today's Japanese youth would hardly think of email as something that happens on a computer (Ito, Okabe, & Matsuda, 2005). To them, mobile email *is* email. There are even some users who would say, "Oh, I didn't know you could do email on a computer." Another popular practice in Japan is using mobile phones as Osaifu-Keitai (mobile phones with wallet functions). People use their mobiles as electronic money, credit cards, electronic tickets, membership cards, and airline tickets (NTT DOCOMO, 2009b). Not surprisingly, much of this activity is infused with location awareness.

Getting GPS directions through car navigation systems is one of the earliest uses of GPS devices in the United States. But the popularity of public transportation in Japan sparked the early development of GPS in handheld devices. A GPS service called NAVITIME, developed in Japan, is a point-to-point route search for both automobiles and mobile devices. The service for mobile devices allows users to plan travel routes with a combination of methods, including walking, driving, and public transportation. The search results show routes combining these methods, allowing the users to compare and choose freely from a variety of navigation routes.

According to the Statistical Handbook of Japan, Japan is the fifth most densely populated country in the world.[3] The country's population density measured 343 persons per square kilometer in 2005, compared with 31 persons per square kilometer in the United States. Shigeyuki *et al.* (2001) concluded that pedestrian trips are positively correlated with population density, which means that the higher the population density, the larger the

Figure 7.1 NAVITIME pedestrian navigation diagram. Photograph © Ian Kennedy 2010, www.flickr.com. Reproduced by permission of Ian Kennedy.

number of pedestrian trips. Thus, unlike GPS applications in the United States that focus on the experience of drivers, the pedestrian-specific navigation application of NAVITIME catered to the heavy pedestrian population, and spearheaded the development of pedestrian-oriented navigation systems.

As a world leader in mobile communication, Japan has developed many of the technologies that have enabled net localities worldwide. Consider i-concier (from the word "concierge"), launched by Japan's largest mobile-phone provider NTT DOCOMO in November 2008. The i-concier mobile application combines GPS, the web, and personal data with artificial intelligence to tailor information to the individual. As NTT DOCOMO envisions it, the device would make the reams of information on smart phones available in a way that integrates seamlessly into people's lives. As you walk into Shibuya in Tokyo on a Sunday afternoon to do a little shopping, for instance, your mobile's software agent, which already knows about your passion for fashion, alerts you to an opening taking place in Daikanyama only a few blocks away. Also, i-concier can notify you of subway breakdowns, traffic accidents and earthquakes, and remind you of local events. It automatically renews digital coupons from restaurants, supermarkets, travel agents, and film distributors that match your particular preferences. You may see a notification on the handset display that informs you of an overdue DVD rental, or that hard-to-get ticket to a Coldplay concert that just went on sale (NTT DOCOMO, 2009a).

The i-concier application is one of several examples of Japanese technologies that seek to connect the web and urban life. Much more than in the United States, Japanese people have been enthusiastic early adopters of these technologies. For this reason, many scholars have looked to Japan to understand patterns of mobile technology use.[4] Japan's pioneering investment in mobile technologies can be attributed to two things. First, since Japan is a small country with limited natural resources, shrinking labor force, and decreasing birth rate, the prosperity of the country is highly dependent on technological advancement (Harayama, 2001). Japan has conservative policies on overseas immigration, which limits its labor force. As a result, it has relied heavily on technologies to provide automation and convenience (Harayama, 2001). Second, the Japanese are comfortable with technologies (Inkster & Satofuka, 2000). This fact might be related to the traditional religion of Shinto, a worship of nature, ancestors, polytheism, and animism, involving honoring and celebrating the existence of Kami, or spirit, essence or deities that are associated with many formats; in some cases human like, some animistic, others associated with more abstract "natural" forces in the world (mountains, rivers, lightning, wind, waves, trees, rocks) (Pilgrim & Ellwood, 1985). This worship blurs the boundaries between perceptions of living things and nonliving things, generally contributing to a more positive approach to technology. The Japanese people have historically been much quicker at embracing and appropriating technologies into their daily lives as fears of losing oneself in the machine have not been prominent in Japanese culture.

China

China is a very different story. Even though China and Japan are neighbors, the context in which location-aware technologies are used and appropriated differs greatly. According to statistics released by the Chinese Ministry of Industry and Information Technology, by the end of 2009 there were 710.5 million mobile phone users in China, 360 million Internet users, and 192 million mobile Internet users. These numbers are staggering as they have increased exponentially over the past decade. Because of this rapid growth, China has become one of the most important markets for mobile phones and the web (*TRENDSnIFF*, 2009). The Open Door Policy in 1978 has facilitated fast economic development in China and has led to a significant increase in the country's urban population. More and more, the Chinese are leaving the countryside and heading to emerging mega-cities that have become centers of global commerce. This of course has contributed to the adoption of mobile technologies and the production of net localities. Different from Japan's free market, China's market is heavily centralized and its media use heavily surveilled. The unique circumstances of the country's markets and culture have created very particular local conditions from which media get adopted in general, and from which net localities form, in particular.

For the past 20 years, perhaps the greatest migration in human history has been underway in China, as rural residents move to urban areas in search of a higher standard of living and employment opportunities. The United Nations projections indicate that China will add 310 million people to its urban areas over the next 25 years, a figure equal to the population of the United States. Along with this rapid influx of population, Chinese cities have undergone massive construction, expansion, and renovation. Old downtown communities in urban centers have been demolished, narrow laneways have broadened, one-storey houses have been replaced with high-rise buildings, and local teahouses are juxtaposed with McDonald's.

This radical transformation of Chinese cities has created unique and troubling conditions for urban residents. Physical space is in constant flux,

Figure 7.2 The first McDonald's in China. It opened on October 8, 1990 in Shenzhen, Guangdong Province, China. Photograph © Eric 2007, http://creativecommons.com.

and information about those spaces is also in flux. Where one socializes, buys groceries and how one travels between nodes in an urban network cluttered with construction, are always changing. The cities in which people reside now are dramatically different from the cities with which they were familiar a decade ago. Combine these conditions with the rise of broadband and mobile web and it presents a clear path toward net locality.

In September 2005, China's largest search engine provider, Baidu, launched the first localized map search service in the country. Following Baidu, in February 2007 Google launched a similar service that provided basic local mapping information (roads, major buildings, bus stations), named Google Maps China. Since then, more and more local information has been added to these mapping services. Chinese web users can now easily search for information about restaurants, banks, hospitals, and Internet cafés within certain geographical areas on either Baidu or Google Maps China. In fact, some mapping websites have enabled users to generate content for web-GIS maps and virtual worlds by uploading and later retrieving differentiated place-specific data (such as photographs, videos, and articles), which are available as "placemarks" on the map. The website

Mapbar.com is a good example. Registered users on Mapbar can create their own maps with themes. Users can create maps or simply click on the themed maps in which they are interested. For example, the map entitled "Shi Yuan Chi Bao" (eating one's fill with less than ¥10), is a collection of inexpensive restaurants. Or, "Laser Strike" documents all the places one can play the popular live action shooting game.

With Mapbar albums, users can upload and share pictures of places they have been, identify these places on maps, and add information such as captions, addresses, and contacts. Thus, each picture of a physical location becomes an informational node in a spatial network. Furthermore, Mapbar enables users to create "points of interest" (POIs) which are identified on maps. The website displays all the newly added POIs from places all over the country.

The case of Mapbar exemplifies the interconnections between social and technological infrastructures (Dourish & Bell, 2007). User generated maps create an infrastructure for users to make sense of their environment. Instead of asking someone where the bookstore was relocated, for example, users can now find all the bookstores within a specific geographic range. Another example is the location of KTVs (also called "karaoke boxes" – establishments in which participants rent out rooms with karaoke equipment). This has become a very popular search string on Mapbar. The technological infrastructure of the map enables a relative path through the objectively shifting physical and informational terrain of the city. While the functionality of Mapbar is no different from many of the mapping applications we have discussed in this book, the way it is used and interpreted is associated with the peculiar cultural context of China.

In China, networking technologies are under centralized control of the government, including the web and mobile phones. Government-controlled firewalls extensively censor the content of online information and mobile text messages (SMS) – something that has both constrained and enabled users' appropriation of these technologies. The Golden Shield Project, a censorship and surveillance technology operated by the Ministry of Public Security (MPS), a division of the Communist government in China, is used to block and filter information on the web and in text messages. Under the system, popular social networking sites such as Twitter, Facebook, and Picasa are banned because of the dangers of spreading anti-government messages and discussions on sensitive topics such as Tibet and Taiwan. The project, which is unofficially referred to as the "Great Firewall of China," traces, scans, and blocks unwanted information based on a list of predetermined "sensitive" words concerning the government or pornography. The list of "sensitive" words keeps changing. For example, when a series of riots and demonstrations took place in the

Tibet Autonomous Region in March 2008, "Tibet" became a sensitive word as it was frequently used in discussions and news coverage of the Tibetan Independence Movement and the boycotts of the upcoming Beijing Olympics. Also on the list is "Tiananmen," the name of the large plaza near the center of Beijing, because the search for this word leads to online information about the Tiananmen Square Massacre, the government's brutal suppression of pro-democracy protests in 1989. It has become a rather well known example that, before Google relocated its servers to Hong Kong, an image search on http://google.cn for "Tiananmen" produced not one tank or display of totalitarian control. Under these circumstances, Chinese netizens invented alternative designations to circumvent the surveillance of the firewall. During the Tibet turmoil, for instance, users replaced the word "Tibet" with a variety of substitutes based on the pronunciation, romanization, and meanings of the original word. As Tibet ("xi zang") in Chinese means the western frontier, one substitute was "dong zang" meaning the eastern frontier. Another substitute was the descriptive phrase "the plateau on the West." These circumventions were local in nature. In order to successfully create content and share information within the network, one had to have sufficient local knowledge to circumvent the database algorithms.

But this centralized control has contributed to the unique manifestation of net localities in China. For example, many municipal governments use a database that contains all mobile phone numbers of people who live in the city. They set up a public text messaging terminal and send one-to-all messages for various administrative purposes. During the Beijing Olympics, for example, the Beijing municipal government frequently sent messages to all mobile users within the city, notifying them of temporary transportation issues. Currently, mobile phone users who take an intercity trip receive automatic text messages as soon as they enter a new city. Typically, the text messages welcome them to the new city and provide local information such as places of interest, weather forecasts, and available accommodations. The government-initiated one-to-all text messaging is a unique manifestation of net localities enabled by the centralized authority in the country. The local technological practices reflect the cultural orientation of collectivism and group decision-making (Hofstede, 2001).

This cultural orientation has lent itself to a robust use of net localities in the neighborhood context. Tiantongyuan (天通苑) is an apartment complex and neighborhood in northern Beijing's Changping District that was established in 1999. As of July 2009 it had over 600,000 residents, and it is the largest of such complexes in Asia. Residents of Tiantongyuan all have access to a website called Jiazhu Tiantongyuan (家住天通苑), which means "living in Tiantongyuan."[5] The website was set up in 2000 by the

Tiantongyuan realtor, and it was started as a real estate information-sharing platform for people buying apartments and settling down in the area. However, it became a platform for addressing public concerns in 2001, when residents used the site to pool money to hire experts to test the drinking water. It turned out the water was extremely polluted. Through the site, the residents were able to amass large groups of people to assemble and petition the media and the mayor of Beijing. Eventually, the mayor was pressured into responding to their needs and the water was treated and cleaned.

Similarly, in 2005, when Beijing Subway Line No. 5 was being built, Tiantongyuan residents staged another campaign. According to the original planning of the subway line, the highly populated Tiantongyuan was to have only one station. As many residents commute from Tiantongyuan to downtown on a daily basis, they asked for another station. Ten residents formed a special action group, and encouraged all residents to "make at least one phone call to one of the government institutions to express the need," or "mail at least one petition letter," or "write at least one petition email" (Shan, 2008). Related government contact numbers were put online; ready-to-be-sent letters were available online for people to download and print; residents were called on to utilize all possible networks and resources to make their voices heard. Through online notification, the special action group organized a below-the-line petition signing that gained more than 10,000 residents' signatures. The signed petition letter was sent to the Beijing Municipal Government. Within months, the second subway line station in Tiantongyuan was approved. Jiazhu Tiantongyuan's success soon became known nationwide, and according to some media critics, was "a miracle in the history of community democratic movements" (Lin & Zhou, 2009).

On July 11, 2009, Jiazhu Tiantongyuan was disabled. On the website's main page, there are a few lines that vaguely explain the reasons for the site's demise: "Based on instructions of the bureau and departments, Jiazhu Tiantongyuan needs to conduct internal rectification. During the rectification period, all services will not be available. We apologize for the inconvenience" (literal translation from the original Chinese text). It was widely believed that the Chinese government had shut down the website because "undesired discussions" (dissatisfaction with the community, criticism of the inefficient government work, etc.) often appeared on the site. However, while it was functioning, Jiazhu Tiantongyuan changed the way local people engaged in community activities. Jiazhu Tiantongyuan set up a model in China for engaging in local issues through online portals, resulting in collaborative activities ranging from grassroots organizing to directly negotiating with the government. Before Jiazhu Tiantongyuan, such activities in

Figure 7.3 The Tiantongyuan subway station. Photograph © Qinwen 2007, http://creativecommons.com.

China had been rare if not completely absent. The use of the website as a local political platform transcended the initial intent of the site.

Many people thought that the web had the capacity to democratize China by granting its citizens access to global information. But what happened with Jiazhu Tiantongyuan was just the opposite. The power of Jiazhu Tiantongyuan was not its connection to the outside world of information; the threat was the ability for the locality to organize and mobilize around very specific local issues. In Jiazhu Tiantongyuan, the openness of the web was directed inward. Net locality reorganized the tactics of control employed by the centralized state. While China's government continues to keep a watchful eye on emerging technologies, the use of the web and mobile devices for local organization will continue to influence how the Chinese construct their local lives. Net locality in China is developing in response to centralized control that seeks to manipulate both the local and global practices of the web.

Considering the Net-Local Future

Net locality is transforming social interactions across the globe. As more and more people have access to location-aware technologies, urban spaces are adjusting accordingly. What happens on sidewalks, plazas, and shopping malls is no longer limited to physical interactions. The sharing of personal data between devices is becoming central to the structure of interactions that daily transpire in urban spaces. And the sharing of information on the web is increasingly organized around the specificity of urban spaces.

Networked localities create a context that allows communities to share more information and resources, and to more effectively plot local knowledge into urban spaces. These practices are increasingly addressing local needs, optimizing the social and cultural appropriation of location-aware technologies. And, as a result, making the human users of those technologies, themselves location aware. Based on "old" web media, the community organization enabled by Jiazhu Tiantongyuan in China demonstrates the political power of net localities. The platform, originally intended to push news to residents, was transformed into a neighborhood network that ultimately empowered people to organize against a negligent government. Residents in Tiantongyuan were able to directly communicate with each other in ways not possible before, and as a result, they transformed their neighborhood through direct and powerful communication with local and national government.

Web and mobile platforms have been often used for spontaneous political organization and protests in different parts of the world. This phenomenon has been called "macro-coordination," that is, mobilizing social networks in public spaces via mobile phones for collective action.[6] The downfall of the Philippines' president Joseph Estrada in 2001 has become the paradigmatic case of macro-coordination. The people in Manila, equipped with mobile phones, sent text messages and email to spontaneously self organize a protest against the president. Networked communication facilitated local action with local consequences.

A similar act of macro-coordination took place during the summer of 2009, when Iranian citizens assembled in Tehran's city center to protest the results of the presidential election. As Iranians took to the streets to register their dissatisfaction with the apparent inaccuracies in counting the votes, many of them used Twitter to share opinions, location of protests, or observations of violence. The space of protest was a net locality. It extended to engage a non-proximate audience. And being connected to the world was necessary for the local event. Not only did the technology help to broadcast the violence to a sympathetic pro-democracy audience worldwide, it also facilitated local actors to act efficiently in a local context.

These local events were of interest to a global audience because of the network. In Iran, the news story was Twitter, not the political context of

Figure 7.4 Pro-democracy protests in Tehran, Iran were partially organized and publicized through Twitter. Photograph © Milad Avazbeigi 2009, http://creativecommons.com.

the protest. Some prominent journalists and commentators referred to the events as the "Twitter revolution" (Ambinder, 2009; Grossman, 2009). Indeed, this moniker has been bolstered in its own Wikipedia entry. But as there were less than 10,000 Twitter users in Iran with fewer than 100 of them active during the events (the spike in activity came from users re-tweeting all over the world) (Schectman, 2009), there is no doubt that the mainstream media's fascination with the "Twitter revolution" is not about political revolution, but about the revelation that a mere social network could be so powerful. The media coverage was about the networks that undergird politically contentious localities.

What does it mean that protesters are connected? What does it mean that the marginalized spaces of the developing world can so quickly self-organize and reach the mainstream? Net localities have become big news precisely because they have demonstrated that they can bypass the mechanisms of local governments and major news outlets. They are a wake-up call for those invested in globalization; the local still matters, and in fact, it may matter more than ever before because it can have an immediate and powerful global impact.

Net localities are always produced in the context of social and political forces because they extend beyond the limitations of mere physicality or mere virtuality. Again, Jiazhu Tiantongyuan became a threat to the government because it fomented local descent through digital connections. The threat was the possibility of local macro-coordination and the potential sympathetic ear outside the geographic location. The strength and flexibility of these connections are transformative for the physical spaces in which people live. The effects of net locality on the physical environment are contingent on the local social and political context. Augmenting existing social connections with networked data can transform the existing social relations that define localities. The busy Tokyo street, the Beijing housing complex, the people in Tehran: each is a unique social situation that, when networked, produces unique results. The local has become global; but the way in which the global produces the local is still very much a local matter.

Notes

1 Early versions of this chapter were co-written with Jean Wang.
2 As Henri Lefebvre (1991) argues in *The Production of Space*, space is a social product, a complex social construction based on values, and the social production of meanings that affects spatial practices and perceptions. Lefebvre posited that spaces incorporate social practices. Every society, and thus every mode of production, produces a certain type of space – its own space. Accordingly every society produces and appropriates particular types of technologies and interactions with digital networks.
3 This report was issued by the Statistics Bureau of Japan.

4 For examples of this research, see Ito, Okabe, & Matsuda, 2005; Rhein-gold, 2002; Okada, 2005; Miyata *et al.*, 2005.
5 See www.tty.com.cn, last retrieved November 1, 2010.
6 Rheingold, 2002; Bimber, Flanagin, & Stohl, 2005; Rafael, 2003; Castells *et al.*, 2007.

References

Ambinder, M. (2009, June 15). The revolution will be Twittered. *The Atlantic*. Retrieved November 1, 2010 from http://politics.theatlantic.com/2009/06/its_too_easy_to_call.php

Bar, F., Pisani, F., & Weber, M. (2007 April). Mobile technology appropriation in a distant mirror: Baroque infiltration, Creolization, and cannibalism. Paper presented at the Seminário sobre Desarrollo Económico, Desarrollo Social y Comunicaciones Móviles en América Latina, Buenos Aires, Argentina.

Bimber, B., Flanagin A., & Stohl, C. (2005). Reconceptualizing collective action in the contemporary media environment. *Communication Theory, 15*(4), 365–388.

Canclini, N. G. (2001). *Consumers and citizens: Globalization and multicultural conflicts*. Minneapolis: University of Minnesota Press.

Castells, M. (2000). *The rise of the network society*. Oxford: Blackwell.

Castells, M., Fernández-Ardevol M., Qiu, J., & Sey, A. (2007). *Mobile communication and society: A global perspective*. Cambridge, MA: MIT Press.

Couclelis, H. (2007). Misses, near-misses and surprises in forecasting the informational city. In Miller, H. J. (Ed.), *Societies and cities in the age of instant access* (pp. 70–83). Dordrecht, The Netherlands: Springer.

de Souza e Silva, A., Sutko, D. M., Salis, F., & de Souza e Silva, C. (in press). Mobile phone appropriation in the favelas of Rio de Janeiro, Brazil. *New Media & Society, 12*(1).

Donner, J. (2005, May). *The rules of beeping: Exchanging messages using missed calls on mobile phones in sub-Saharan Africa*. Paper submitted to the 55th Annual Conference of the International Communication Association, New York, pp. 26–30.

Dourish, P., & Bell, G. (2007). The infrastructure of experience and the experience of infrastructure: Meaning and structure in everyday encounters with space. *Environment and Planning B: Planning and Design, 34*(3), 414–430.

Farley, T. (2005). Mobile telephone history. *Telektronikk, 3*(4), 22–34.

Gibson, W. (1984). *Neuromancer*. New York: Berkley.

Goggin, G. (2006). *Cell phone culture: Mobile technology in everyday life*. New York: Routledge.

Grossman, L. (2009, June 17). Iran protests: Twitter, the medium of the movement. *Time*. Retrieved November 1, 2010 from http://www.time.com/time/world/article/0,8599,1905125,00.html

Harayama, Y. (2001). Japanese technology policy: History and a new perspective. *REITI Discussion Paper Series,* 01-E-001. Tokyo: Research Institute of Economy, Trade and Industry.

Hofstede, G. (2001). *Culture's consequences: Comparing values, behaviors, institutions, and organizations across nations.* 2nd edn. Thousand Oaks, CA: Sage.

Inkster, I., & Satofuka, F. (2000). *Culture and technology in modern Japan.* New York: I. B. Taurus.

Ito, M., Okabe, D., & Matsuda, M. (Eds.). (2005). *Personal, portable, pedestrian: Mobile phones in Japanese life.* Cambridge, MA: MIT Press.

Lefebrve, H. (1991). *The production of space.* Oxford: Blackwell.

Lin, T., & Zhou, K. (2009, July 1). The growing of Tiantongyuan. *China Youth Daily.* Retrieved November 1, 2010 from http://www.cyol.net/zqb/content/2009-07/01/content_2736346.htm

Meyrowitz, J. (2005). The rise of glocality: New senses of place and identity in the global village. In Nyíri, K. (Ed.), *A sense of place: The global and the local in mobile communication* (pp. 21–30). Vienna, Austria: Passagen Verlag.

Miyata, K., Boase, J., Wellman, B., & Ikeda, K. (2005). The mobile-izing Japanese: Connecting to the internet by PC and webphone in Yamanashi. In Ito, M., Okabe, D., & Matsuda M. (Eds.), *Personal, portable, pedestrian: Mobile phones in Japanese life* (pp. 143–164). Cambridge, MA: MIT Press.

MSNBC. (2005, October 7). A cell phone that points to Mecca: "Ilkone" reminds Muslims of 5 daily prayer times. *MSNBC,* Technology and Science section. Retrieved November 1, 2010 from http://www.msnbc.msn.com/id/9622362/

NTT DOCOMO. (2009a). "i-concier" service heralds age of personalization. *NTT DOCOMO Mobility Quarterly.* Retrieved November 1, 2010 from http://www.nttdocomo.com/binary/press/mobility_doc_24.pdf

NTT DOCOMO. (2009b). What's "Osaifu-Keitai"? NTT DOCOMO official website. Retrieved November 1, 2010 from http://202.214.192.60/english/service/convenience/osaifu/about/

Okada, T. (2005). Youth culture and the shaping of Japanese mobile media: Personalization and the keitai internet as multimedia (pp. 41–60). In Ito, M., Okabe, D., & Matsuda, M., (Eds.), Personal, portable, pedestrian: Mobile phones in Japanese life. Cambridge, MA: MIT Press.

Orwell, G., (1949). *1984.* New York: Rosetta Books.

Pilgrim, R., & Ellwood, R. (1985). *Japanese religion.* 1st edn. Englewood Cliffs, NJ: Prentice Hall.

Rafael, V., (2003) The cell phone and the crowd: Messianic politics in the contemporary Philippines. *Public Culture, 15*(3), 399–425.

Rheingold, H., (2002) *Smart mobs: The next social revolution.* Cambridge, MA: Perseus.

Schectman, J. (2009, June 17). Iran's Twitter revolution? Maybe not yet. *Bloomberg Business Week.* Retrieved November 1, 2010 from http://www.businessweek.com/technology/content/jun2009/tc20090617_803990.htm?chan=top + news_top+news+index+ - +temp_news+%2B+analysis

Shan, H. (2008, January 9). Residents urge rail access. *China.org.cn*. Retrieved November 1, 2010 from: http://www.china.org.cn/english/China/240033.htm

Shigeyuki, K., Satoshi, H., Nobuo, M., Myungsoo, K., Wann, Y., Juneyoung, K., Kiho K., Hyungchul, K., & Hyonnie, L. (2001). Comparison between Japanese and Korean cities from the view of compact city living environment system: Comparative study on the residents' transport behaviour between the Western Area of Fukuoka City and Sungnam City. *Fukuoka University Review of Technological Sciences, 67*, 59–67.

TRENDSnIFF. (2009). China internet users reach 360 mil, mobile internet 192 mil. *TRENDSnIFF Blog*. Retrieved November 1, 2010 from http://trendsniff.com/2009/11/08/china-Internet-users-reach-360-mil-mobile-Internet-192-mil/

8

Conclusion

We are experiencing a fundamental shift in the way we understand physical space. It is no longer independent from digital (networked) space. The web is all around us. We no longer "enter" the web; we carry it with us. We access it via mobile, mapping, and location-aware technologies. It is embedded in all sorts of sensors and networked devices. Mobile phones, Global Positioning System (GPS) receivers, and radio-frequency identification (RFID) tags are only a few examples of location-aware technologies that mediate our interaction with networked spaces and the people in them. When these technologies know where we are, they inevitably influence how *we* know where we are.[1]

Our physical location determines the types of information we retrieve online, and the people and things we find around us. It is true that technologies have become location aware; but it is also true that we have become more aware of our locations. We are more location aware because we are connected in new ways through these technologies to the spaces and people around us. We can attach information to places, map our surroundings, and connect to people around us. Being aware of location means being aware of all the information and people that exist in that location. And it means making different use of that location. Networked interactions permeate our world. And it is becoming increasingly implausible to act as though they do not.

This is net locality. It is a world intimately entwined with the digital networks that stream through it. It is manifesting in everyday social practices like mapping, mobile annotation, and location-based social networks, but it has implications for how we engage with each other and the

Net Locality: Why Location Matters in a Networked World, First Edition. Eric Gordon and Adriana de Souza e Silva. © 2011 Eric Gordon and Adriana de Souza e Silva. Published 2011 by Blackwell Publishing Ltd.

world, even outside of these practices. It affects politics, entertainment, and everyday life.

In this book, we have attempted to put this "new" phenomenon into historical perspective. Net locality has gained influence in the new millennium because of the development of high-speed networks and locative technologies (GPS, Wi-Fi, Bluetooth). But it emerged from a long history of mapping, art, and research. It is not a product of the iPhone or the Droid. It is the product of the social need to locate people and things, and of developing connections based on who and what's nearby. These practices denote different but overlapping ways of locating people, objects, and places via networking technologies; and, in doing so, they also create a framework for the development of new social spaces and community interaction. As these practices become more common, the very nature of physically situated social interaction is transformed. The notion that the web and mobile technologies disconnect us from physical spaces is less and less convincing. Even the novelist William Gibson, the author of *Neuromancer*, and the man responsible for term cyberspace, has admitted this in a September 2010 op-ed in the *New York Times*. "Cyberspace, not so long ago" he says, "was a specific elsewhere, one we visited periodically, peering into it from the familiar physical world. Now cyberspace has everted. Turned itself inside out. Colonized the physical" (Gibson, 2010). The web and the world it occupies can no longer be separated.

We live in net localities. These spaces will continue to influence how we interact with each other on a local and global level, and how we delimit the borders around our own personal space. In this book, we have addressed the social implications of net localities for the way people interact with their local communities, local governments, and each other. We have also explored the fears and concerns that arise when nearly everything might be locatable. People living in net localities will need to reconsider not only how they understand public spaces, but also private spaces. Personal location, once considered a private matter, can now be broadcasted to a network of friends, and to companies that will target users with advertising. Net localities are commodified spaces. They are not fundamentally different from traditional "offline" urban spaces, but they clearly reorient the urban dweller into an urban consumer. The network empowers the individual; we have detailed this phenomenon in the book. But it also delivers the individual into a highly rationalized consumer space where the distinction between consuming and being is blurring.

Net localities are enabled by technologies; but they are produced through social interactions. We have tried to clarify throughout this book that despite the global reach of the web, it still maintains its local specificity. Furthermore, similar technological infrastructures are socially appropriated in different ways, leading to the subsequent development of distinct net localities in several parts of the world. So, while it is likely that urban spaces will grow increasingly networked, individual localities will be able to maintain their cultural, political, and social characteristics.

But much of this remains unpredictable. Technology is continually changing at a faster and faster clip. Net localities are currently produced through a variety of technologies such as desktop computers, geographic information system (GIS) mapping, mobile phones, and GPS – all of which are connected via cellular networks, the internet, and short range signals like Bluetooth and Wi-Fi. These technologies have created the framework that produced net localities, but it would be short sighted to define this phenomenon through them. That would be as absurd as defining televisions as a box with vacuum tubes.

As of this writing, in Fall 2010, this infrastructure is changing. And although it is not our intent to predict the future, the current state of technological development leads us to believe that increasingly there will be no purpose in differentiating between mobile phones and personal computers, or between televisions and game consoles – or even between refrigerators and cars, since all will become interfaces that connect us to the web and to people and things around us. As objects in the world (including people, places, and things) are integrated into the web, any distinction between the world and its information will fall away.

Technological Infrastructures

The expansion of net localities has been hastened by the rapid development of fourth generation (4G) networks. This 4G technology is most typically known as an extension of current third generation (3G) services. The 3G mobile phones are capable of fast connection speeds and constant data transfers. They allow users to connect to the web, stream videos, and download applications at much higher speeds than former second generation (2G) phones – which were basically just used for calls and SMS. The 4G phones are even faster than the 3G ones, and capable of even larger data streams (Saveri, Rheingold, & Vian, 2008). But mobile phones were not always capable of connecting to the web.

Although a commercial mobile phone service has been around since the late 1970s,[2] mobile phones only acquired internet connection capabilities when 2G was released, in the early 1990s. At that time, however, connection was circuit switched, which meant that customers had to pay for the amount of time they were connected. And because connection speeds were very slow, accessing the web via a mobile phone was expensive. As a consequence, very few people actually used their mobile phones for anything more than voice and SMS. This started changing when 2.5G phones came out in the late 1990s, although 2.5G was not really a new standard. It used a system called GPRS (General Packet Radio Service) that ran on a particular kind of 2G phone.[3] Besides offering a much faster connection than former 2G phones, GPRS phones allowed users to connect to the web via packet switched technology, which means that users paid for the amount of data they used – rather than the amount of time they used. Building on this platform, the Wireless Application Protocol (WAP) was one of the first technologies that sought to provide users with a seamless interface to the web. But WAP fell short of users' expectations. Mobile-phone users in the United States and Europe were used to accessing the web via a desktop computer, in the comfort of their homes or offices, on a big screen. For many users, WAP just didn't feel like the web.

In Japan, however, the story was different. NTT DOCOMO invested very early in the mobile web. The i-mode standard, used in Japan since late 1990s, provided phones with constant connection to the web. But technological practices are never disconnected from social practices. The i-mode standard was so successful in Japan because, among other reasons, most young Japanese first connected to the web via their mobile phones. Without previous experience with PCs, they did not perceive what they did with their phones as "entering the web," but just as another function of their *keitais* (the word for mobile phone in Japanese) (Rheingold, 2002; Ito, Okabe, & Matsuda, 2005). Additionally, NTT DOCOMO made it very easy for i-mode users to create and upload their own mini-webpages to the i-mode network.

The possibility of user-generated content is one of the main reasons for the popularity of the web (Jenkins, 2006a, 2006b; Shirky, 2008). And it was no different with mobile phones. It is not surprising, then, that the first 3G phone was released in Japan. Shortly after its release, 3G spectrums were auctioned in the United Kingdom, and other European countries, followed by the United States. Although 3G networks promised fast network connection speeds and the ability to download and stream video and audio to mobile devices, early 3G customers were disappointed (Wilson, 2006). The extraordinary price paid by providers for 3G spectrums was transferred to 3G services, which were offered at very expensive rates and mostly failed to meet user expectations. Furthermore, providers adopted a top-down approach, making it very difficult for users to create their own mobile web content and mobile applications.

But attitudes started to change with the introduction of user-friendly operating systems (such as iPhone and Android) that enabled users to create their own mobile applications and easily interact with and produce content to the mobile web. And of course, as content become located and locatable, the potential of the mobile web became obvious. Still, even though cellular networks are quite fast now, and mobile phones have become small computers, these phones are still commonly viewed as "just phones."

In early 2009 several mobile phone companies started to announce the launch of 4G phones, which promised faster connections and seamless integration between devices.

But 4G technology was not fully available. Most of the technology branded as 4G at the time used standards like LTE (3GPP Long Term Evolution) or WiMax (a type of long-range wireless network), which did not fully comply with 4G standards. While a single mobile phone is able to handle connections through an increasing number of networking technologies (LTE, Wi-Fi, RFID, Bluetooth, and others), they are still kept separate in actual practice. Mobile phones do not automatically switch to the best technology depending on what is available in its location. According to technology scholar Simone Frattasi, so far there is no convergence of networks. Networking technologies (Wi-Fi, cellular networks) are confined to specific devices and applications. For example, Wi-Fi is still generally used in laptops, while cellular networks are the default wireless technology for mobile phones.

The tendency is that mobile phones will be able to connect to the web with increasing speeds, but at this point consumer prices are still very high for high-speed mobile networks to take off.[4] But even when they do, the way mobile phone companies advertise 4G networks (focusing on phones) misses the big picture of what might be ahead of us. The 3G but faster model of 4G networks is what Frattasi *et al.* (2006) describe as a "linear 4G vision." The real potential of the 4G infrastructure, however, lies in what they call the "concurrent 4G vision," which is not simply about improving coverage and spectral efficiency, capacity, and reliability (Katz & Fitzek, 2006; Javaid *et al.*, 2008), it is about enabling communication across platforms and services. A core characteristic of 4G is that it induces different types of devices able to connect with each other and share information and resources. One example is the current use of intelligent transport systems (ITS) to plan vehicle routes and traffic management (Javaid *et al.*, 2008). ITS have been around for many years, but more recently megacities in Asia, North America, and Europe have implemented a new generation of ITS that includes, among other things, integrated fare management and traffic prediction. New ITS take advantage of location-based technologies that connect transportation systems to users' mobile devices. As a result, they can alert passengers when the next bus is coming, deviate traffic flows, suggest new travel routes based on real time traffic information, and manage an integrated system of fares and parking prices (Houghton, Reiners, & Lim, 2009). The goal of ITS is to seamlessly integrate GPS-equipped public and private transportation networks (buses, subway, airplanes, cars, bikes) with users' location-aware mobile communication technologies within an intelligent management system.

These systems mark a shift in how we understand the web: no longer merely a digital network enabled by TCP/IP that connects servers and routers across the globe, but also a convergence of networking practices that start at the local level, connecting different types of networks (Wi-Fi, WiMax, Bluetooth, WiBro, and Mesh networks), and different types of devices (mobile phones, cars, buildings, sensors, tracking devices, and appliances).

The cooperative platform envisioned by concurrent 4G includes a large range of devices, networks, and services, building on the ubiquitous computing paradigm originally proposed by Mark Weiser in the early 1990s at Xerox PARC (Palo Alto Research Center). The idea of ubiquitous computing suggests that each user is served by tens or hundreds of computational devices, located not only on the desktop, but spread throughout the environment (Weiser, 1991). In ubiquitous computing, the site of interaction with computation is the physical world. The ubiquitous computing paradigm forces us to think about computers in a different way: no longer the personal computer on a desktop, but all types of electronic devices, sensors, and services available to us in our environment. Adam Greenfield (2006) notes that the development of Weiser's initial idea went off track during the decade that followed its invention. Instead of sticking to a general concept that considered the overall integration of computational elements into our physical world, much of the post-PC research and development community focused on several narrow areas, such as context-aware computing, mobile computing, wearable computing, situated computing, and so forth. But in doing that, they were missing the big picture and the common elements that integrate all these technologies. Additionally, he argues, from the perspective of the general user, people mostly experience an ecology of devices and platforms, most of which have nothing to do with our original idea of "computer" as a desktop PC. In other words, we don't care what tool we use as long as it works efficiently. We don't care where we access the web, as long as it is intuitive, user friendly, and non-disruptive. Greenfield suggests we need a new term that touches on this computing ecology. He calls it "everyware" (2006, p. 17).

But terms like ubiquitous computing or everyware designate the development of *technological infrastructures*. Although these terms are concerned with the user experience of technology, they mostly describe the types of technologies used for providing networked connections. For this reason, they are different from net locality. Net locality is a cultural shift in the way we experience our spaces and social connections. It is supported by the development of ubiquitous computing infrastructures, but it is really about what happens to us, our society, and our spaces once this infrastructure is in place.

Social Infrastructures

We produce our technologies and our technologies produce us (Turkle, 1995). Technologies are shaped by the places and localities in which they are located (Dourish & Bell, 2007). So we cannot just look at technological infrastructures, we have to look at social infrastructures, or the social context of technology use. For example, in Asia, social and governmental control often dictate how technology is used (Bell, 2005). SMS filtering software enacted by the Chinese government, national mobile and web censorship regulations and practices in Singapore, and strict limits put over mobile phone use by religious groups in Malaysia and Indonesia all demonstrate that technology is a product of where it is and the institutions that contain it.

But infrastructures are not only digital technologies. Physical plans and traffic flows, service times and density, are all infrastructures that shape one's experience of space and social life. With the rise in the number of people that work from home full time in the United States, for instance, infrastructures that facilitate the lives of telecommuters are in great demand. Home-based workers will eat in local restaurants, go to farmers' markets, attend fairs and festivals, and read local weekly newspapers. Local life is a product of local events, institutions, and cultures.

It is this dependence on local knowledge, the increasingly strong sense of local identity and the corresponding social behaviors and preferences, that shapes the forms and planning of local facilities. This is where net locality comes in. Mobile phones and GPS devices facilitate social mobility as they provide communication and connection to places. At the same time, they are socially appropriated. Communication and connection to places varies in style and function. GPS owners need to constantly update maps from the network to obtain the most recent location-based information, such as new facilities or road blocks. The practice of text messaging changes depending on the local context. In India, fishermen out at sea use text messages to learn about the demand on shore, and therefore channel their catch to the right port (*Lanka Business Online*, 2009). In Kenya, people pay for airfare, train tickets, and bus tickets via text message (Constantinescu, 2009). In Uganda, farmers frequently find answers to questions about farming practices and health issues using Google text messaging and an operator service (Arnquist, 2009). Mobile technologies are as much cultural and social objects as they are technological objects (Nugroho, 2002; Ozcan & Kocak, 2003). Since different cultures and societies have different values, expectations, and practices, net localities will always vary from culture to culture, society to society.

Moving Forward

As the web becomes ubiquitous and embedded in physical space, there is a need to understand the growing importance of locality. On the one hand, we might think that national boundaries are eroding, and cities are losing their unique characteristics. Indeed, as Castells (2009) observes, there is "a crisis of the nation-state as a sovereign entity" (p. 39). But, at the same time, "nation-states, despite their multidimensional crises, do not disappear; they transform themselves to adapt to a new context" (p. 39). This new context is net locality. The fact that the web is marching steadily along the path to localization is an indication that local communities, cultures, and contexts have always been relevant, and always will be. It would be naive to deny the influence of global networks on local communities. However, what we can observe now, in perhaps comparable intensity, is the influence of local knowledge and local information in shaping global networks. It is in this tension between the local and the global that net locality unfolds.

Net locality changes the meaning and value of the web, not because the technology has determined that to be the case, but because people have adopted networked technologies for local purposes. After roughly 20 years of existence, it is clear now that the web needs to be understood in its local context. The time has passed for comparing virtuality and physicality. We do not leave our bodies, even momentarily, for digital interactions. And increasingly, we do not leave the context of our locality in order to interact with and within digital networks. We exist in communities, neighborhoods, networks, and spaces. The global networks that enable these interactions shape the conditions, but they do not produce meaning. Meaning is produced locally.

Notes

1 Early versions of this chapter were co-written with Jean Wang.
2 For more on this, see Farley, 2005; Agar, 2004; and Goggin, 2006.
3 In particular, it worked on a GSM (Global System for Mobile Communication) 2G.
4 Simone Frattasi, personal communication, August 25, 2010.

References

Agar, J. (2004). *Constant touch: A global history of the mobile phone*. Duxford, UK: Icon Books.

Arnquist, S. (2009, October 5). In rural Africa, a fertile market for mobile phones. *The New York Times*, Science section. Retrieved November 9, 2010 from http://www.nytimes.com/2009/10/06/science/06uganda.html

Bell, G. (2005). The age of the thumb: A cultural reading of mobile technologies from Asia. In Glotz, P., Bertschi, S.,& Locke C. (Eds.). *Thumb culture: The meaning of mobile phones for society*. Bielefeld, Germany: Transcript Verlag.

Castells, M. (2009). *Communication power*. Oxford: Oxford University Press.

Constantinescu, S. (2009, October 23). *People in Kenya can now buy flights and bus tickets with their mobile phone; I wish I was joking*. Retrieved November 9, 2010 from http://www.intomobile.com/2009/10/23/people-in-kenya -can-now-buy-flights-and-bus-tickets-with-their-mobile-phone-i-wish-i-was -joking.html

Dourish, P. & Bell, G. (2007). The infrastructure of experience and the experience of infrastructure: Meaning and structure in everyday encounters with space. *Environment and Planning B: Planning and Design*, *(34)* 3, 414–430.

Farley, T. (2005). Mobile telephone history. *Telektronikk*, *3*(4), 22–34.

Frattasi, S., Fathi, H., Fitzek, F.H.P., Prasad, R., & Katz, M.D. (2006). Defining 4G technology from the users' perspective. *IEEE Network*, *20*(1), 35–41.

Gibson, W. (2010, August 31). Google's Earth. *The New York Times*. Retrieved November 9, 2010 from http://www.nytimes.com/2010/09/01/opinion/ 01gibson.html

Goggin, G. (2006). Making voice portable: The early history of the cell phone. In *Cell phone culture: Mobile technology in everyday life* (pp. 19–40). New York: Routledge.

Greenfield, A. (2006). *Everyware: The dawning age of ubiquitous computing*. Berkeley, CA: New Riders.

Houghton, J., Reiners, J., & Lim, C. (2009). Intelligent transport: How cities can improve mobility. *IBM Global Business Services*. Somer, NY: IBM Corporation.

Retrieved November 9, 2010 from ftp://public.dhe.ibm.com/common/ssi/ecm/en/gbe03232usen/GBE03232USEN.PDF

Ito, M., Okabe, D.,& Matsuda, M. (Eds.) (2005). *Personal, portable, pedestrian: Mobile phones in Japanese life* (pp. 123–142). Cambridge, MA: MIT Press.

Javaid, U., Rasheed, T., Meddour, D., Ahmed, T., & Prasad N. R. (2008). A novel dimension of cooperation in 4G. *IEEE Technology and Society Magazine*, Spring, 29–40.

Jenkins, H. (2006a). *Fans, bloggers, and gamers: Exploring participatory culture.* New York: New York University Press.

Jenkins, H. (2006b). Convergence culture: Where old and new media collide. New York: New York University Press.

Katz, M. D., & Fitzek, F. H. P. (2006). Cooperation in 4G networks: Cooperating in a heterogeneous wireless world. In Fitzek, F. H. P., & Katz, M. D. (Eds.), *Cooperation in wireless networks: Principles and applications; real egoistic behavior is to cooperate!* Dordrecht, The Netherlands: Springer.

Lanka Business Online, (2009, October 7). Mobile phones ring in growth in emerging markets. *Lanka Business Online.* Retrieved November 1, 2010 from http://www.lankabusinessonline.com/fullstory.php?nid=829481534

Nugroho, Y. (2002, August 12). Addiction to mobile phones amid neo-liberalism. *The Jakarta Post.* Retrieved November 9, 2010 from http://www.thejakarta post.com/news/2002/08/12/addiction-mobile-phones-amid-neoliberal ism.html

Ozcan, Y. Z., & Kocak, A. (2003). Research note: A need or a status symbol? Use of cellular telephones in Turkey. *European Journal of Communication, 18*(2), 241–254.

Rheingold, H. (2002). *Smart mobs: The next social revolution.* Cambridge, MA: Perseus.

Saveri, A., Rheingold, H., & Vian, K. (2008). Technologies of cooperation: A social-technical framework for robust 4G. *IEEE Technology and Society Magazine*, Summer, 11–23.

Shirky, C. (2008). *Here comes everybody: The power of organizing without organiza-tions.* New York: Penguin.

Turkle, S. (1995). *Life on the screen: Identity in the age of the internet.* New York: Simon & Schuster.

Weiser, M. (1991). The computer for the 21st century. *Scientific American, 265,* 94–104.

Wilson, J. (2006). 3G to web 2.0? Can mobile telephony become an architecture of participation? *Convergence: The International Journal of Research into New Media Technologies, 12*(2), 229–242.

Index

Net Locality: Why Location Matters in a Networked World, First Edition. Eric Gordon and Adriana de Souza e Silva. © 2011 Eric Gordon and Adriana de Souza e Silva. Published 2011 by Blackwell Publishing Ltd.